the truth about babies

From A-Z

IAN SANSOM

Granta Books

London

Ian Sansom lives in Ireland with his wife and children (not pictured).

'Draws multiple voices, from the Bible to Nabokov, into his own funny, on-the-job reflections on the bottom, soul, and infinite paraphernalia of his baby son, nicely disproving the cant which says that it is only this generation of fathers who have concerned themselves with the mewlings and pukings of their offspring' Rachel Polonsky, *Evening Standard*

'*The Truth About Babies* is a sort of joyful *Waste Land*: the book Eliot might have written if he and Vivien had abandoned Pound and perplexity and gone shopping for prams. Like Barthes, Sansom has a light touch with the weightiest of subjects . . . delightful' *Irish Times*

'Sansom's observations about parenthood are extremely perceptive, very sharp and often funny' *Junior*

'The soundbite format rocks you into its meditative rhythm and it's great for any parent who wants to snatch some intelligent reading . . . non-parents can enjoy the historical, literary and philosophical quotes' *Herald*

contents

preface

These notes and stories, compiled between birthdays, in the years 1997–2001, some time after dark and before dawn, sometimes at the end of the bed or on early-morning train journeys, in bus stops and waiting rooms, but mostly in the kitchen drinking coffee during nap times listening to the radio at low volume, are not at all what I intended.

What I intended, of course, what I'd hoped for, was a big book, and a book written at a desk, or a lectern perhaps, written during the hours of daylight probably, and worthy of comparison with the best of the works of world literature, with *The Epic of Gilgamesh* maybe, and *The Egyptian Book of the Dead*, with *The Mahabharata* and Homer, with the Hellenistic Greeks, with the great poetry and prose of Europe and America, with Alfred Lord Tennyson, say, and the essays of Ralph Waldo Emerson, with M. Scott Peck and with Melville, with good old Piers the Plowman, and with Penelope Leach.

The book I intended was to be at least as useful as Dr Spock, as beautiful as the twenty-three-volume Zervos catalogue of Picasso, and as essential to good living as the works of W. H. Auden and *The Simple Solution to Rubik's Cube*.

You see, when you think about babies you don't think small. You think big. When you think about beginnings you soon get to thinking about immortality.

The book I intended was encyclopaedic, comprehensive and definitive. It exists, that book, in a set of calf-bound thread-sewn manuscripts, the paper as thick as it is cream, with gold on the spine and rose on the edge, written with a Mont Blanc in purple ink, and also on the hard-disk drive of a state-of-the-art Apple Macintosh laptop computer. It bears no sign of crossings-out, second thoughts, uncertainties or stylistic equivocations. It is so large, so utterly in and of itself, that it contains everything and yet leaves no room for others. It ranks as literature and bears the comparisons, yet is utterly *sui generis*.

Alas, there is no such manuscript book and no laptop. My notes are all in blue, black and red biro, corrected in soft pencil, written on scraps of paper kept under the bed in a brown shoebox ('Genuine Dr Martens Air Wair Air-Cushioned Comfort', 'BLACK 7 EYE') inscribed on the lid in red felt-tip, 'BABY, NOTES'. There are frequent doodles in the margins.

So what happened? What went wrong?

We had a baby. And babies are not aware of good intentions. They affect your plans and your purposes and they don't allow you much time for reading and writing, never mind producing a masterpiece. Or it may be that I was just in too much of a hurry, or too lazy. Anything more, though, and anything longer, would have seemed like a weariness and an obstruction, and there are plenty of those already. The bookshops are full of them, the shelves overflowing, and when we first had a baby and still had money in our pockets I could not find a single baby book that I wanted to read.

I found that I didn't want a manual or a reference book, and I didn't want a joke book. I didn't want pictures. I didn't want a book about fatherhood or motherhood, I didn't want a novel, and I definitely did not want an anthology of poems. I did not want advice, and I did not want other people's complaints, or statements of their own good intentions. I didn't want sludge, slurry, emotional slither, or sentimentality. I didn't want to be patronized, and I didn't want self-help. I didn't want Technicolor, but I didn't want black and white either. In fact, I don't think I really wanted a book about babies.

I think what I wanted, what I was after, was some kind of benediction, but I also wanted someone to tell me the truth. I wanted someone to make the true seem beautiful and the beautiful true — just the usual.

I wanted feeling, then, and conscience, and I wanted the effect of actuality. I wanted someone to capture the charm of a person. I wanted a book that had the attraction of fiction with none of its disadvantages: characters, plot, long plodding descriptive passages. I wanted more than a pious statement of hopefulness — more than a preface. More than a catalogue of experiences. I wanted no aesthetic mistakes.

I still haven't found it.

This is the alternative.

It didn't take long, and it took for ever. The children are still young, but the rest of us are getting older, and I don't know how that happened at all. It's not what we intended, but it's the best we can expect. I'm sure the other book is out there somewhere, so maybe if you find it, you could let me know?

Thanks.

advice

Never feed raw meat to a baby. If you're standing up, sit down, and if you're sitting down, lie down. A piece of soft white bread rubbed on the wallpaper will take away most stains.

With a baby, everybody's an expert, but nobody wants to tell you what to do. It's like a secret.

Except, there is no secret.

Or it's like the Freemasons' secret: just an apron and a mallet.

It's like becoming an adult all over again, or a teenager: the sudden realization that everyone is pretending, and nobody really knows what to do. It's a shock. We need reassurance.

There is none.

It takes a while, but after about three months we realize that there is no answer to the question, 'Are we doing it right?' We're just doing it.

At first we wanted someone to tell us what to do: that would make it easy.

But after a while we become expert in you.

You're like an instant hobby. You're like smoking. Or religion.

You get to be very *ex cathedra* with a baby.

I ask my mum if she has any advice.

She says yes, certainly she has. 'Always finish the washing-up before you go to bed.' Good advice.

ageing

You age quickly – within days. Your skin darkens and roughens. Your nails toughen. It's like watching paint dry, crack and peel, all in the space of a week.

At the same time you unwrinkle. I'm amazed. It's like someone's blowing you up. It's like watching a time-lapse natural history documentary in reverse.

You seem to be simultaneously disintegrating and expanding.

You plump up.

'Plump', in the OED: '"Fat", rich abundant; well-supplied; full and round in tone; great, big; complete, round'. But also, 'To fall, drop, plunge, or come down (or against something) flatly or abruptly (usu. implying "with full or direct impact")'.

You're six weeks old. We return from a visit to my parents, late at night, in torrential rain. When we open the front door there's the sound of running water. Part of the roof of the flat has caved in. I shout. You scream. It's way past midnight.

Over time the natural environment acts upon the outer surface of a building in such a way that its underlying materials are broken down. This breakdown, when left to proceed uninterrupted, leads to a failure of materials and the final dissolution of the building itself – ruination – hardly an outcome desired by the architect, builder or owner. In order to prevent this or retard its occurrence buildings must be maintained. Maintenance, in most general terms, aims at renewal and involves both conservation and replacement. So costly has this process become nowadays that buildings are designed to be maintenance-free, or to require as little repair as possible. Nevertheless, no matter how maintenance-free the construction, weathering still occurs.

Moshen Mostafavi and David Leatherbarrow,
On Weathering (1993)

I decide to change before dissolution sets in.

I believed for years – for years I believed this – that doing something I didn't want to do was a good excuse for not doing something I wanted to do. Does that make sense?

ambitions

James Boswell in his diary reacts to the birth of his son in 1775:

> When I had seen the little man I said that I should now be so anxious that probably I should never again have an easy hour. I said to Dr Young with great seriousness, 'Doctor, Doctor, Let no man set his heart upon any thing in this world but land or heritable bonds; for he has no security that anything else will last as long as himself.' My anxiety subdued a flutter of joy which was in my breast. I wrote several letters to announce my son's birth. I indulged some imaginations that he might perhaps be a Great Man.

Boswell imagining a Great Man: he could do no other. It was his life's work: Dr Johnson was his baby.

People either want a Boswell, or they want to be a Boswell.

We all like to indulge ourselves, believing our friends and family to be extraordinary: awful, treacherous, generous or kind. Thus, 'We have a terrible baby', or 'We have a wonderful baby.'

All parents exaggerate. No one wants their children to be uninteresting. (Or their emotions about their children.)

Of course we would like you simply to be happy, to be contented.

But we would also like you to be the first Taoiseach of a united Ireland. (Stella Tillyard, in her book *Aristocrats*, tells the story of Henry Fox and his son Charles – 'Fox lifted Charles up on the table and put him on top of a prize joint of roast beef so that the child could sit astride the symbol of England itself, a living image of Fox's hopes for his sons.' So what should we do? Pose you with potatoes?)

Actually, we wouldn't mind you becoming a good plumber. Or neighbour.

You know the story of the three tailors? The first tailor puts up a sign in his window that says, 'We tailor the best clothes in Ireland.' The second tailor takes up the challenge and puts a sign in his window that reads, 'We tailor the best clothes in the world.' The third tailor is now faced with a problem. After much thought he puts up a sign in his window: 'We tailor the best clothes in this street.'

Where we live there are no tailors. Maybe this is an opportunity.

Siegfried Sassoon, after the birth of his son George, wrote to his friend Max Beerbohm in November 1936: 'Will he, I wonder, become Prime Minister, Poet Laureate, Archbishop of Canterbury, or merely Editor of *The Times Literary Supplement*? – or Master of the Quorn? Or merely the Squire of Heytesbury?'

We like to kid ourselves that the achievement of ambitions requires only the exercise of skills and charm, but everyone knows this isn't true. There is no necessary correlation between busyness and success.

It's all down to luck. It's down to your parents.

anecdotes

Parents thrive on anecdotes, like dissidents on samizdat. Parents are gossips and speculators. They are day-traders.

You leave clues. You feed us a line. You leave us to fill in the gaps.

We have a slug, or a snail, who comes out from the skirting at night. He leaves frenzied trails on the rug. We never see him and can never catch him, even with saucers of beer.

I'm worried about you catching something from the slime.

But at least it's not mice, or rats.

With babies, there's no time for fooling around with narrative, with niceties like beginnings and middles and ends. You have no plot. You're pure story. You defy the stylistic conventions.

You are not a character 'in the round'. Your behaviour appears contrary to logic.

And you do not speak. You supply none of the usual dialogue prompts and bubbles.

'I fancy mankind may come, in time, to write all aphoristically, except in narrative; grow weary of preparation, and connection, and illustration, and all those arts by which a big book is made' – James Boswell, quoting Johnson, *Journal of a Tour to the Hebrides with Samuel Johnson* (1785).

I find myself collecting anecdotes, like droppings.

angel

I really don't like people calling you 'angel'.

It makes you sound like you're dead already.

'Darling' I don't mind, or 'gorgeous'. But 'pet', no.

Charles Péguy was opposed to 'angelism': the seeking of salvation elsewhere.

anxiety

Books about infant and child psychology are like those maps by ancient geographers who concealed their lack of knowledge with pictures of strange animals. They do not represent the real world. They don't show true directions. They illustrate only the fears and anxieties of the map-makers.

Roll up the map. It will not be wanted.

For example, Melanie Klein, 'On Observing the Behaviour of Young Infants' (1952), from Envy and Gratitude (1975):

> The new-born infant suffers from persecutory anxiety aroused by the process of birth and by the loss of the intra-uterine situation. A prolonged or difficult delivery is bound to intensify this anxiety. Another aspect of this anxiety-situation is the necessity forced on the infant to adapt himself to entirely new conditions.
>
> These feelings are in some degree relieved by the various measures taken to give him warmth, support and comfort, and particularly by the gratification he feels in receiving food and in sucking the breast. These experiences, culminating in the first experience of sucking, initiate, as we may assume, the relation to the 'good' mother. It appears that these gratifications in some way also go

towards making up for the loss of the intra-uterine state. From the first feeding experience onwards, losing and regaining the loved object (the good breast) become an essential part of infantile emotional life.

Whatever we might say about you is only ever the same as what we might say about life after death.

There is no MRI scanner for the soul.

There is no MRI scanner for the home.

At the beginning of *Bonanza*, the map bursts into flames.

apgar test

Your first test.

Named after the American anaesthetist Virginia Apgar, who devised it in the 1950s.

You pass. I'm delighted. I say, 'Well done.'

You are half an hour old.

I wish I hadn't said it.

I don't want you to spend your whole life collecting gold stars.

a p p e a r a n c e

It takes about three months for a baby to start to look like a baby.

When you are first born you are at what H. L. Mencken calls the 'larval stage' of life. You do not look like a baby. You look like a very large maggot.

Actually, you don't just look like a maggot.

You never look the same from one day to the next, or from one perspective or another. You seem to contain within yourself multiple personae. From behind you look like an old man, from the side, like a pregnant woman. You look alternately wise and simple, old and young, male and female. Some people say you look like x. Other people say you look like y. They are both right. You are inconsistent. You lack an identity. You are not yet possessed of self-sameness.

Ralph Waldo Emerson, in 'Fate', from *The Conduct of Life* (1860):

> In different hours, a man represents each of several of his ancestors, as if there were seven or eight of us rolled up in each man's skin, – seven or eight ancestors at least, – and they constitute the variety of notes for that new piece of music which his life is. At the corner of the street, you read

the possibility of each passenger, in the facial angle, in the complexion, in the depth of his eye.

In an airport departure lounge I'm sitting next to a Buddhist monk. In purple robe and saffron vest. His skull is dolichocephalic rather than brachycephalic. He turns to talk to his colleague. He's Glaswegian.

I work with someone who turns out to be a high priest of a coven.

I work with someone else who turns out to be very nice.

Appearances deceive. According to Josephus, Jesus was short, hunchbacked, with a scanty beard and eyebrows that met in the middle.

Your appearances deceive. You are smiling contentedly, gurgling. You look lovely. I pick you up to cuddle. From behind you're soaked, from the neck down, in a mustardy slick of shit and piss.

My appearances deceive. I am maintaining the illusion of a normal life.

I bite into a shiny supermarket nectarine – two days old. We have a dozen in a netted plastic punnet. The flesh is like sawdust.

attention

You demand attention. But attention is one of the many things I no longer have: fresh shirts, clean sheets, dignity. My attention span has gone out on me.

In the park, a father, his young son about to go down the slide.

His mobile rings.

The boy starts crying, arms outstretched at the top of the slide.

baby monitor

There are two channels, A and B. For weeks we stick with A, and happily eat our dinner to the sound of your steady breathing.

Turned up all the way, whacked up to the max, the noise is incredible. The feedback, it's like Hendrix. It's better than white noise. It's stentorophonic.

Then one night, the monitor picks up the sound of a musical mobile.

You do not have a musical mobile.

We rush into your room, terrified, choking on our food.

You lie there, peaceful, silent, sleeping.

There are no demons or thieves, no Pied Piper tempting you away.

But there are voices on the monitor, talking. We listen. It sounds just like us, but it's not us.

Someone else in the street must have a baby and a monitor.

We dutifully switch to Channel B.

Sometimes, secretly, I switch back.

I miss them out there on Channel A: they're like part of the family.

We see our *doppelgängers* out on the street sometimes. We smile. I want to introduce myself. I've heard their baby breathing. And it sounds exactly the same.

b a d

At five months, in our eyes, you can still do no wrong.

So when does it happen? When do you start doing wrong?
When do you become a 'bad' baby?

William Hazlitt:

> A great but useless thinker once asked me, if I had ever
> known a child of a naturally wicked disposition? and I
> answered 'Yes, that there was one in the house with me that
> cried from morning to night, for *spite*.' I was laughed at for
> this answer, but still I do not repent it. It appeared to me
> that this child took a delight in tormenting itself and others;
> that the love of tyrannizing over others and subjecting them
> to its caprices was a full compensation for the beating it
> received, that the screams it uttered soothed its peevish,
> turbulent spirit, and that it had a positive pleasure in pain
> from the sense of power accompanying it.

Do you deliberately torment yourself and others with your
crying?

Do you set out to irritate and annoy?

Can you make mistakes even?

No, no, and three times no.

The experience of the baby is close to the experience of a god, or the genius.

'A man of genius makes no mistakes. His errors are volitional and are the portals of discovery,' says Stephen Dedalus discussing Shakespeare in *Ulysses*.

On your first birthday you try to bite my mum. I shout, 'No! Naughty boy!'

baldness

You're bald. And I'm balding. There seems to be only so much hair to go around.

> 62
> The clock
> on the bookcase ticks,
> the watch on the table ticks –
> these busy insects
> are eating away my world.

> 63
> My hair was caught in the wheels of a clock
> and torn from my head: see, I am bald!
>
> Charles Reznikoff,
> *Jerusalem the Golden* (1934)

The sheets give you the tonsure.

If everyone slept long enough and still enough, we'd all of us be monkish.

William Empson: 'A monk oughtn't to have a baby, but somebody else has to have babies, if only to keep up the supply of monks.'

bathing

There is no danger of emptying the baby with the bathwater. It's not like boiling potatoes.

You love being in the water. We bath you in the sink, in the washing-up bowl and in a red plastic toolbox.

Water arouses a great excitement and sometimes a great anxiety in you. You laugh, and then you cry.

Perhaps you are exhibiting what Sandor Ferenczi calls the 'thalassal regressive' tendency, associating water with the waters of the womb and with man's pre-human development, what Ferenczi calls a 'striving towards the aquatic mode of existence abandoned in primeval times'.

Perhaps not.

But when we lay you on the bed on a towel after a bath you flap around like a landed fish, and when lying on your stomach you wave your arms and legs as if swimming.

Me, I find myself bathing more. I have stopped biting my fingernails and I have regular haircuts. I eat fewer large meals, but more biscuits. I add a late-night snack of crackers and cheese. The moderate enjoyments are more valued: stirring shit-stained clothes in a plastic bucket in the bath, for example, at midnight, listening to Jazz FM.

21

beauty

They say beauty is its own excuse.

But it's difficult to admit how beautiful you are. It is impossible to admit to our admiration. I am English and excellence of any kind embarrasses. I have to make a joke of it. I have to make excuses. I can't even tell my friends.

'X and Y are pleased to announce . . .'

What I want to do is announce you the way George E. Belmont announced Marie Lloyd at the Sadler's Wells Theatre back in 1895: 'Tasty, Trippy, Twiggy, Timely, Telling, Tender, Tempting, Toothsome, Transcendent, Trim, Tactical, Twinkling, Tricksy, Triumphal, Tantalizing'.

What I do is type up details of your date of birth and your weight and use the photocopier in the post office.

Do you want to know why you're beautiful?

You are beautiful because you are not concerned with your own beauty. Hölderlin, on childhood: 'Es ist ganz was es ist, und darum ist es so schön' ('It is wholly what it is, and therefore it is so beautiful').

The slug trails on the rug look like glue and glitter.

beginnings

You are constantly beginning: smiling, eating, moving, crawling. You seem to have a purpose.

And this makes us think we have a purpose too. Which is crazy, when you think about it. We do not have a purpose. And neither do you.

You are eight months old before I manage to work out what this means.

You may not have a purpose, but this does not mean you are purposeless. On the contrary. You have no purpose because your beginning will have no end. You are superfluous.

'When will you make an end to it?' demands Rex Harrison as Pope Julius II in *The Agony and the Ecstasy* one afternoon, while you're having a nap and I'm supposed to be working. Charlton Heston is playing Michelangelo, painting the Sistine Chapel ceiling on our portable telly. 'When I am finished,' replies Michelangelo to the Pope, Charlton to Rex.

You are four months old. On the train, passing through Hornsey into King's Cross, there is a Christmas tree, with lights, in someone's front room. It is 21 January.

birth

Like the Emperor Caligula, Gore Vidal claims that he can remember being born:

> I am in a narrow tunnel, wriggling toward the light, but I get stuck before my head is free of the tunnel. I cannot move forward or backward. I wake up in a sweat. Nina's pelvis was narrow and I was delivered clumsily, with forceps, by a doctor not used to deliveries: he was officer of the day in the Cadet Hospital at West Point, on a Saturday, October 3, 1925, at about noon.

There are very few reliable accounts of how we are born.

Most people see a birth maybe once or twice in a lifetime, in situations in which they are either in too much pain or too emotionally involved to be relied upon for evidence. Birth therefore remains a mystery.

But would you want witnesses?

> It was relatively late in life that [Margaret] Mead became a mother, her daughter being born when she was thirty-eight. The previous afternoon, Margaret had finished writing an article for the *Encyclopaedia Britannica*, just as her own mother had finished writing an article for the *Encyclopaedia Britannica*

before giving birth to her. But in Margaret's case there was the kind of commotion she found it second nature to create. Howard describes the delivery as being 'delayed for ten minutes until the arrival of the photographer'. It was 'witnessed by the obstetrician, several nurses (all of whom, at Mead's request, had seen the Bateson–Mead film "First days in the Life of a New Guinea Baby"), a child development psychologist, a movie photographer, and the paediatrician Dr Benjamin Spock'. Significantly the father, Bateson, was elsewhere.

Liam Hudson and Bernadine Jacot,
Intimate Relations: The Natural History of Desire (1995)

Some friends video the birth of their first child. After dinner one night, after a couple of bottles of wine, they invite us to watch the video with them. I'm disgusted. Really, appalled. I feel as though we have been invited to participate in group sex.

I look up the strange and unnatural births famously listed by Pliny in his *Natural History*, Book 7, Chapter 3: Bacchus engendered through Jupiter's thigh; Minerva through Jupiter's brain; Adonis out of a myrtle tree; Castor and Pollux from the shell of an egg laid and hatched by Leda. And there are others: Pallas out of a skull; Persilis from a drop of holy water; Arimaxus from a hole in the ground; Leucomedon, the son of a cavern in Mount Aetna.

Reality is stranger still: a giraffe has to drop about one and a half metres to the ground when it is born; cuckoos famously lay their egg in other birds' nests, and the cuckoo chick that hatches first then shoves out all the others.

You corkscrew out, at speed, head first.

When you come out you look like a good Stilton: wrinkled brown coat and a blue-veined creamy body. I think – I really think this – you look good enough to eat.

I watch the video. They have added a soundtrack.

Gore Vidal is a liar.

blemishes

At about six weeks blemishes appear on your body, red patches with a white frosting or scurf on your back and your arms and legs, like eczema.

I'm worried you may never make it as a rabbi, or a priest (Leviticus 21:20 excludes from the priesthood the man who has 'a continual scab or dry scurf in his body').

We rub oil into your skin. The blemishes vanish. Thank the Lord.

blue

We dress you in blue. For male babies, blue is obligatory. Blue means masculinity. It is the colour of achievement: the blue ribbon.

The term 'cordon bleu' originally designated a knight of the Order of the Saint Esprit, founded by Henry III on the occasion of his accession to the throne of France, and was so named according to the colour of the ribbon from which the cross of the Order was suspended.

Blue: indubitably male.

But blue also the colour of the Virgin Mary, the colour of religion and mystery (Numbers, chapter 15 verse 38: 'Speak unto the children of Israel, and tell them to make to themselves fringes on the borders of their garments, putting in them ribbons of blue').

Colours do not represent ideas.

b o d y

All the parts of you are close together.

You're so compact, when we hold you in our arms we can feel your whole being beating under the skin, like a cat. It's scary.

You look perfect. But of course, compared to an adult, you're all out of proportion. Your head is too big: about one-quarter of the total size of your body (in adults the proportion is about one-eighth).

Your eyes are too big.

Your forehead is enormous.

Your cheeks are puffy.

You're a freak.

In Mervyn Peake's pencil drawings of his young children they look like startled monsters. Indeed, he calls them 'Forsaken monsters shouldering through my mind'. The drawings are all mouths and eyes: staring, disturbed, strange.

In *A Zoologist Looks at Humankind* (1990), Adolf Portmann explains that 'Human torsos, arms, and legs must each cover a completely different developmental trajectory to reach the size of the adult state; the proportions in the human newborn are completely different from those of the mature form.'

We are obsessed with bodies. The body has replaced God as an object of fascination: bodies keep us occupied.

Mary Douglas, in *Purity and Danger* (1966):

> The body is a model which can stand for any bounded system. Its boundaries can represent any boundaries which are threatened or precarious. The body is a complex structure. The functions of its different parts and their relation afford a source of symbols for other complex structures.

Example: 'The map of Ireland', according to William Trevor in *A Writer's Ireland* (1984), 'is not unlike a sleeping infant: the rounded head of Ulster, fingers scattered to make the islands and inlets of the West, toes spread out in Dingle and the O'Sullivan country, Carnsore Point the tip of the spine.'

In the mirror I stare at the faltering outline of my own body. I am coming to resemble the shape of mainland Britain.

books

The experts disagree.

But experts always disagree.

> There is nothing which is not the subject of debate, and in
> which men of learning are not of contrary opinions. The most
> trivial question escapes not our controversy, and in the most
> momentous we are not able to give any certain decision.
> Disputes are multiplied as if everything was uncertain.
>
> David Hume, *A Treatise of Human Nature* (1739–40)

Elizabeth Gaskell, writing in 1835 about her six-month-old
daughter Marianne, lamented that the 'Books do so differ'
(although she does say that her favourite child-care book –
'quite the nicest book on the subject' – was Albertine Necker
de Saussure's *Progressive Education*).

The only true book is a recipe book.

As with recipe books, we soon realize that we can combine a
few of the ingredients, add whatever we've got in the
cupboard, substitute some Schwartz dried herbs for the fresh
and make it up ourselves.

In books about babies, as in almost all books – let's leave aside
the King James version of the Bible – the quantity of

information bears an inverse relationship to the quality of explanation.

There are only two kinds of useful writing about babies: textbooks and poems.

There are in fact only two useful kinds of writing.

I am pushing you around a bookshop, and it suddenly occurs to me that I no longer wish to read or possess books. It is enough simply to know that they are there. I think I understand now why my mother never read books. She didn't even have a Dr Spock.

The only book I now desire is a book which covers roofing, vermin-killing, magic tricks and the preserving of supermarket soft fruits.

I have given up on fiction. Fiction is tinned meat. Novelists add ice to cheap wine to diminish its crudity. I desire the actual: ham on the bone. No water added.

Slowly but surely our books are losing their bindings.

boredom

You can be boring.

Sorry.

Me too.

bottle-feeding

They call it 'formula'-feeding. Compared to the breast it sounds scientific, chalked up, modern.

Churchill, in a speech on the radio on 21 March 1943: 'There is no finer investment for any community than putting milk into babies.'

But putting milk into babies is expensive. Margaret Thatcher got rid of milk from schools, to save money. She withdrew the breast.

Along with the nappies I calculate that the milk costs us nearly £15 a week.

Bottles with plastic nipples were not in use until the nineteenth century. Before that, feeding vessels were made of horn, glass, pottery, wood, porcelain and leather. These were known variously as sucking bottles, pap-boats and bubby-pots. The teats were sometimes made of a calf's nipples pickled in spirit.

You don't start to grow fat until you're formula-feeding. You swell up, as if you're eating junk food. In your sleep-suits you look like a Las Vegas Elvis.

And from about twelve weeks you tap out a finger signature on the bottle as you're feeding.

boy

Even at six months your face is sexually undefined. People say, 'Is he a boy or a girl?'

In later life this confusion is virtually impossible. It's very rare that one meets someone whose sexual identity is not immediately discernible, and when one does it's shocking.

For at least the first six months of life you are like an androgynous deity.

Peter Ackroyd, writing about transvestism: 'If, as the Creation myths assert, Chaos – or the unity of undifferentiated sexuality – is the progenitor of life, then the separate sexes represent a falling off from that original fecundity. Androgyny, in which the two sexes coexist in one form and which the transvestite priest imitates in his own person, is an original state of power.'

True story: you're six months old, and I'm on the train on the way to work. A woman opposite me is wearing a grey feather boa. She has peroxide blonde hair.

I am reading a book – Tony Parsons, *Man and Boy* – a book so bad it makes me want to cry. I am too tired to read books any more: even good books irritate me, and bad books leave me enraged.

The woman in the feather boa is also reading a book. I glance across to see what book she is reading – it's something by Mario Vargas Llosa. I am intrigued. Everyone else on the train is reading *Man and Boy* by Tony Parsons. I look a little longer. I notice the woman's hands.

They are a man's hands.

The man/woman wears thick black tights. She has a beautiful black leather handbag at her feet, from Paris (the clasp says 'PARIS').

breast-feeding

On the breast you seem to be in Paradise. The food you
require reaches unto you – as in Marvell's poem 'Thoughts in
a Garden':

> What wondrous life is this I lead!
> Ripe apples drop about my head;
> The luscious clusters of the vine
> Upon my mouth do crush their wine;
> The nectarine and curious peach
> Into my hands themselves do reach;
> Stumbling on melons as I pass,
> Ensnared with flowers, I fall on grass.

It is amazing. People watch. They can't help it.

Sometimes you bang the side of your head against the breast.
And you shout with contentment when you have the nipple in
your mouth. You suck the nipple right to the back of your
mouth, and then use your tongue to squeeze milk into your
throat.

I put my finger in your mouth, to see what it's like. Your
gums clamp around my finger, hard. I let you lick at my
fingers. It is ticklish, exciting. Your tongue loops round,
curls.

When you finish feeding and you want to sleep your tongue protrudes between your lips and you hold the fingers of your right hand splayed. You're satisfied. You're safe (the breast as defence, the *mamelon*, the fortified mounds forming one of the defences of Sebastopol during the Crimean War).

Freud, in 'Three Essays on the Theory of Sexuality' (1905): 'No one who has seen a baby sinking back satiated from the breast and falling asleep with flushed cheeks and a blissful smile can escape the reflection that this picture persists as a prototype of the expression of sexual satisfaction in later life.'

Freud had some odd ideas. The expression may be the same, but this does not make the experience similar or prototypical. A resemblance is not an identity.

According to Valerie A. Fildes in her monumental history *Breasts, Bottles and Babies: A History of Infant Feeding* (1986) — an amazing book — in ancient Egypt, 'Breast milk was included in many oral remedies and local applications for a variety of conditions, including retention of urine in a child; for expelling noxious excrements in the belly of a man; burns, erysipelas, and eczema.'

Apparently, puppies, children and attendants used to suck off the excess milk. Or mothers used to manage it themselves, using sucking glasses, which were shaped a bit like pipes: the orifice placed on the breast and the pipe turned upwards towards the mouth, the milk collecting in the bowl.

Writes Fildes:

> During this period [1500–1800] fears about sagging and scarred breasts were a reality for all women, as evidenced by the many pages which midwifery writers devoted to diseases of breasts and nipples and to their remedies. It was

apparently not unusual for women who breast-fed to lose their nipples completely, either because of repeated cuts which became infected and left disfiguring scar tissue, or because hungry older children (equipped with teeth) chewed them off.

She writes also about nipple shields made from hollowed nutmegs, which makes me think of Shakespeare. I don't know why.

b r e a t h i n g

You do not seem to suffer from bad breath.

But you snore.

Sometimes it sounds as though you have crumbs, or perhaps a ping-pong ball, or – no – yes – maybe even an oyster stuck in your throat.

(Thackeray, for reasons that have never been clear to me, compared the experience of swallowing an oyster to swallowing a baby. The texture, I wonder, or the taste?)

> Will you please rush down and see
> ma baby. You know, the one I talked
> to you about last night
>
> What was that?
>
> Is this the baby specialist?
>
> Yes, but perhaps you mean my son,
> can't you wait until   ?
>
> I, I, I don't think it's brEAthin'
>
> > > William Carlos Williams,
> > > > 'To Close'

buggies

No one pushes prams any more, apart from the rich and the poor: those who have inherited. The only pram-pushers I've seen recently are gypsies – in Uxbridge, in Norfolk, and beside the motorway in Belfast.

Everyone else is pushing buggies.

No one will inherit buggies. Buggies are made of lightweight metal and plastic. After about a year the wheels fall off and the frame begins to bend – with all that weight, they seem to go soft.

Unless your arms are very short, you have to hunch to push a buggy. And if you have long legs you have to shuffle.

The pram-pusher is upright and elegant, wrists concealed.

But you can only push a buggy like a barrow.

My mother's gran, Gran – we all called her Gran, although she was dead twenty years before I was born – pushed a barrow, selling second-hand clothes on the streets of Bethnal Green. My parents always refer to it as her 'tot' stall.

My father's grandfather kept a goat on the landing of the buildings where he lived, not far from Bethnal Green, and he built a cart, and the goat pulled the cart carrying the children. When the children got too old for the cart they ate the goat.

The first perambulator, I read, was a miniature carriage built for the third Duke of Devonshire – it was drawn by a dog. There have also been petrol-engined prams.

I am pushing my own tot stall up the hill on the way home, with eight carrier bags of shopping from the supermarket slung from the handles. The bags are carefully balanced. It's raining – sheeting down. Water is running down on to you from the crap, ripped rain-cover. You are screaming. It is only 10.30 in the morning. I haven't done last night's washing-up.

I need dogs.

I need my great-grandfather's goat.

I need petrol.

I need a pot of coffee, or hot fresh tea, or a bottle of steaming cold vodka. Anything.

Nabokov, in *Speak, Memory* (1967):

> You know, I still feel in my wrists certain echoes of the pram-pusher's knack, such as, for example, the slight downward pressure one applied to the handle in order to have the carriage tip up and climb the curb. First came an elaborate mouse-gray vehicle of Belgian make, with fat autoid tyres and luxurious springs, so large that it could not enter our puny elevator. It rolled on sidewalks in slow stately mystery, with trapped baby inside lying supine, well covered with down, silk and fur; only his eyes moved, warily, and sometimes they turned upward with one swift sweep of their showy lashes to follow the receding of branch-patterned blueness that flowed away from the edge

of the half-cocked hood of the carriage, and presently he would dart a suspicious glance at my face to see if the teasing trees and sky did not belong, perhaps, to the same order of things as did rattles and parental humor. There followed a lighter carriage, and in this, as he spun along, he would tend to rise, straining at his straps; clutching at the edges; standing there less like the groggy passenger of a pleasure boat than like an entranced scientist in a spaceship; surveying the speckled skeins of a live, warm world; eyeing with philosophic interest the pillow he had managed to throw overboard; falling out himself when a strap burst one day. Still later he rode in one of those small contraptions called strollers; from initial springy and secure heights the child came lower and lower, until, when he was about one and a half, he touched ground in front of the moving stroller by slipping forward out of his seat and beating the sidewalk with his heels in anticipation of being set loose in some public garden. A new wave of evolution started to swell, gradually lifting him again from the ground, when, for his second birthday, he received a four-foot-long, silver-painted Mercedes racing car operated inside by pedals, like an organ, and in this he used to drive with a pumping, clanking noise up and down the sidewalk . . .

Not for the first time in my life, and for a variety of reasons, I think, I am not in the same class as Nabokov.

You are one year old, we're returning from a party. The frame of the buggy finally snaps outside the Tube station. We get a cab. It's your first taxi ride.

A friend, an American, is struggling to get his baby son into a buggy. He says, 'Keep your seats for the next ride.' It has no effect on the baby, but it makes me laugh.

43

buttons

Buttons are bad. Poppers are good. For everyone buttons are a fiddle.

> Pray you, undo this button   *King Lear*, Act 5, Scene 3

Buttons become gendered.

I have never before been interested in fabrics and fastenings, but now I'm forming opinions: nylon is bad; popper studs are good; buttons are best. Zippers are OK but they're cruel. Zippers catch.

Robert Friedel, in his book *Zippers* (1994):

> With its meshing scoops, pulled together by a (one hopes) smoothly running guide, the zipper fits comfortably into the most general image of the machine, that of the meshing gears. The zipper is thus . . . a perfect representative of 'paleotechnic culture' – the phase in material development characterized by metals and mechanisms.

carpets

Some stains are hard to shift. You'd be surprised: shit's not too bad.

The man in the carpet warehouse says, 'Remember, the life of a carpet is not its pile but its weave.'

To my surprise, completely without warning, I have come to care about carpets. I have come to share the opinions of my parents.

'It's not like we're in the Blue Mosque in Isfahan, but would you mind if I asked you to take off your shoes . . .'

I am painting the lino. Is character like a good linoleum seen through a magnifying glass? The design inlaid and going right through to the bottom?

Or is it not? Is it more like bare boards requiring polish?

c a r r y i n g

You can't walk – that's obvious. We have to carry you everywhere.

But even when you can walk, we still have to carry you everywhere.

We live on the third floor of an old mansion block. There's no lift.

My arms grow stronger.

'Have you been working out?' asks a friend. Yes. I have.

Swans ride on their mother's backs. We carry you in a sling. It makes you marsupial – a koala, a kangaroo, an opossum. The sling is made of blue corduroy. People stop us in the street and say they wish they'd had something like that when they were bringing up the little ones. You dads these days, they say. I think it's wonderful what you do.

You're a dead weight.

> As a drenched, drowned bee
> Hangs numb and heavy from a bending flower,
> So clings to me
> My baby, her brown hair brushed with wet tears
> And laid against her cheek;

Her soft white legs hanging heavily over my arm
   Swing to my walking movement, weak
With after-pain. My sleeping baby hangs upon my life,
   Like a burden she hangs on me;
She who has always seemed so light,
   Now wet with tears and pain hangs heavily,
   Even her floating hair sinks heavily
   Reaching downwards;
As the wings of a drenched, drowned bee
   Are a heaviness, and a weariness.

D. H. Lawrence,
'A Baby Asleep after Pain' (1909)

cars

Authentic Being, reasoned Needleman, could only
be achieved on weekends, and even then it required
the borrowing of a car.
          Woody Allen, 'Remembering Needleman'

Cars create and legitimize our rootless, scattered existence
('automobile', from the Greek *autos*, self, and the Latin, *mobilis*,
movable).

Cars make families and destroy them. They define and
legitimize the experience of being a parent, or a provider. They
are a standard piece of family equipment, like Tupperware.

Friends with children tell us they have bought an MPV. I say,
'What is an MPV?' They laugh. What planet am I on? (And
what income bracket am I in?)

They explain.

An MPV is three rows of seats, big windows, an elevated
driving position, reach and rake adjustable steering, fuel-
efficient electro-hydraulic power assistance, steering-wheel-
mounted audio controls, electrically adjustable and heated door
mirrors, electrically operated front sunroof with extra

ventilation, and a big wedgy nose. It is power and responsibility.

It's rubbish. Cars are just metal boxes with motors.

We do not own a car, so we do not feel like proper parents. Buses are not about power and responsibility. A bus is the opposite of a car.

My grandad was a conductor on a trolleybus, the 665, Barking to Bloomsbury. He'd probably have passed by Leonard and Virginia.

He died before you were born. In a dream I imagine asking him, 'Is there room for a small one on top?'

> Most of us, when we drive our cars, willingly accept a degree of risk for ourselves, our wives and children which we would regard as criminally negligent in any other field – the wiring of electrical appliances, say, or the design of a bridge or apartment block, the competence of a surgeon or midwife. Yet the rough equivalent of speeding on unchecked tyres along a fast dual carriageway at the end of a tiring day at the office is lying in a hot bath with a blazing three-bar electric fire balanced on the edge below a half-open window rattling in a rising gale. If we really feared the crash, most of us would be unable to look at a car, let alone drive one.
>
> J. G. Ballard, 'The Car, the Future', from Drive (1971)

We take the chance. We buy a car. It changes everything.

You don't add a car to society and get the same society plus cars. You get a different society.

And you don't add a car to a child and get the same child plus a car. You get a different child. According to Alice Guppy, in her book *Children's Clothes 1939–1970: The Advent of Fashion* (1978):

> Saving of labour was not always the main motive behind the ready acceptance of easy care. . . it was the car which began to dictate baby's life style. Instead of being pushed sedately along the highways and byways baby was whizzing around the country in a car and wherever he went he must be accompanied by his equipment and this had to be adapted accordingly. Where the family went baby went, at home or overseas, unlike the old days when mother was tied to the house with a young child. The travelling baby spurred on the adoption of disposable napkins, and was behind mothers' insistence on simple outfits which could be washed out and dried overnight. Crease-resistance was another advantage when things had to be packed into the boot.

change

You can have no idea what you've done. The changes. They're catastrophic.

'I'm not a man,' wrote Nietzsche in *Ecce Homo* (1908), 'I'm dynamite.'

A boy, in atomic-weapon parlance, is 'a device that explodes successfully. Since 1945 there have been over 200 boys. American boys have been announced on the following occasions: Trinity, Hiroshima, Nagasaki, Crossroads, Sandstone, Ranger, Greenhouse, Buster-Jangle, Tumbler-Snapper, Ivy, Upshot-Knothole, Castle, Teapot, Wigwam, Redwing, Plumb-bob, Hardtack, Dominic' – Donald M. Kaplan and Armand Schwerner, *The Domesday Dictionary* (1964).

chaos

Unscrew the locks from the doors!
Unscrew the doors themselves from their jambs!
Walt Whitman

Coming home from the hospital: the farmhouse descending out of the whirlwind.

'I have a feeling we're not in Kansas any more.'

We weren't prepared for this.

There's no way anyone could be prepared for this.

It feels as though you've outwitted us.

> Mark the babe
> Not long accustomed to this breathing world;
> One that hath barely learned to shape a smile,
> Though yet irrational of soul, to grasp
> With tiny finger – to let fall a tear;
> And, as the heavy cloud of sleep dissolves,
> To stretch his limbs, bemocking, as might seem,
> The outward functions of intelligent man.
> Wordsworth, 'The Excursion', Book 5

Who's moved the furniture?

cheeks

You have Brando's chipmunk cheeks from *The Godfather*.
In fact, in profile you're all cheek.

child-care

A relationship is an arrangement.

And an arrangement should please everybody.

Writing about a baby implies of course that one is not currently looking after a baby, or perhaps not looking after a baby correctly.

And it's true, I am not at this moment puréeing organic vegetables for your meals tomorrow. But it's OK. I've stocked up on jars. And you seem happy watching *Ready Steady Cook*.

For the sake of Holman-Hunt's painting *The Scapegoat* several of the models – the poor goats – were starved to death.

chin

Americans call a tickle on the chin a 'chin-chuck'.

As the weeks and months pass by, you develop a face within a face. At three months you have a double chin.

(So do I: it's the biscuits.)

It suits you, the chin. It makes you look adult, distinguished. It makes you look human.

Edward Landseer: 'No animal but Man has a chin.'

Food collects in your chins and is difficult to dislodge and remove. We wipe our fingers deep under your chin, into the fat.

choices

Choices multiply: when to dress you, when to change you, when to feed you, when to put you to bed, when to wake you, when to let you sleep, which size and brand and type of nappy to buy.

These are puzzles rather than problems. Or they are problems of style.

I used to find it difficult enough deciding what to have for breakfast.

We bicker. We do not argue: an argument requires energy and commitment.

Sometimes it feels as though you are deliberately testing us, waging a war of attrition on our nerves.

I can't understand why it's so difficult, until I realize we are making all your choices for you. We've doubled up.

The burden is extraordinary and out of all proportion, since the nature of the choices is such that they have no real width and no depth. To choose Huggies or Pampers: it's total freedom. It's capitalism. It's awful. It is the Law of Diminishing Concerns.

Reinhold Niebuhr, in one of his 'sermonic essays', 'Childhood and Maturity', in *Beyond Tragedy* (1938):

> The unity of a child's life is akin to animal serenity. The harmonies of nature have not been disturbed in it, though it must be admitted that the youngest human infant reveals elements of freedom which make bovine serenity impossible. The child is not at war with itself. With the growth of reason and the consequent growth of freedom the alternatives which present themselves to human choice grow in bewildering complexity.

Parents might soon be able to choose their unborn child's gender, hair colour, etc.

We had trouble choosing a buggy.

(It's not easy. They come in a range of removable and washable fabrics, with trigger control systems which allow the chassis to fold and lock, foot-covers, rain-covers, muffs, hoods. And some have only three wheels.)

cinema

You are six months old. We go to the cinema. I'd forgotten what I'd been missing.

Not the films.

We can watch films on video. What I'd been missing was automatic weapon fire at high volume and in surround-sound. Blood, sweat, the popcorn, tears. Halitosis. Holding hands.

circumcision

Should we or shouldn't we? My grandmother says, 'Will you have him circumstanced?'

Circumstanced is correct: we wish to impose upon you.

There is a youth's circumcision dress in the Musée de l'Homme, Paris, of stripy brown and yellow. It looks like prison garb. Circumcision is an attribution of guilt – or a guilty act – and an exoneration.

> That pretty little bleeding part
>   Of foreskin send to me:
> And I'll return a bleeding heart,
>   For New-year's gift to thee.
>
> Rich is the gem that thou didst send,
>   Mine's faulty too, and small:
> But yet this gift Thou wilt commend,
>   Because I send Thee *all*.
>   Robert Herrick, 'To His
>   Saviour, The New Year's Gift'

In the hospital, the nurse says, 'You want him circumcised? Find a rabbi.'

J. C. Flugel, in *The Psychology of Clothes* (1930), lists five forms of body modification: cicatrization, tattooing, painting, mutilation and deformation.

You have not been circumcised. We have not cut your skin, or bound your feet. Your body has been neither decorated nor mutilated. You remain unmodified.

Up until 1876 the British Army had letters tattooed on the wrists of bad characters (B C) and deserters (D). It would make life easier, wouldn't it?

clinics

Child welfare began in France, after the Franco-Prussian War (1870–71), when Pierre Budin established his *consultation de nourrissons*, clinics for suckling babies, at the Charité hospital in Paris. The women attended an outpatients clinic every Friday, where their babies were weighed and examined.

Nothing much has changed – except we go on a Wednesday.

At your seven-month assessment the health visitor says, 'That's textbook.'

I congratulate you again.

Damn.

clothes

Beware of any enterprise that requires new clothes.
                                        Henry David Thoreau

Clothes signal and accelerate your development. At two months
you are pure and white, in one-piece suits, all torso, like a
foetus, or a sperm. At seven months you look like a gangsta-
rapper. Soon we will be buying you guns.

We dress you in loose clothes to allow you freedom of
movement. They also imply that you are about to engage in
heavy physical work.

Occasionally, adults dress like babies, although only in
America. Alison Lurie, *The Language of Clothes* (1981):

> The southern resort where I am writing this chapter (Key
> West, Florida) is full of adults dressed as toddlers or even as
> infants. They wear styles identical with those sold in the
> baby departments of stores: elastic-waistband skirts and
> shorts and slacks, polo and T-shirts with easy-off open necks
> and snap closings, and rompers or crawlers (now called
> 'jump suits'). These simple garments are constructed of the
> traditional materials of infant wear – cotton jersey,

seersucker and polyester – and come in the traditional colours: pale pink, pale yellow, baby blue, lime green and white. Often they are printed or appliquéd with whimsical images of birds and beasts, the penguin and the alligator being current favourites.

When you are born you look androgynous: but we quickly begin to pose you in clothes that identify and express your gender. I am surprised at myself, that I dislike so strongly your wearing the 'wrong' clothes.

Flugel again, in *The Psychology of Clothes*: 'There seems to be no escape from the view that the fundamental purpose of adopting a distinctive dress for the two sexes is to stimulate the sexual instinct.'

The way we clothe you is a signal to others not just of who we are (rich, poor, fussy, fun, serious, sloppy), but who we think you are. Do we think you are cute? Then we'll dress you in bonnets and frilly clothes. Do we think you are wild and untamed? Then we'll put you in brightly coloured clothes.

I imagine designing my own clothes for you: bright, loose one-piece suits, like those worn by mental patients. With no buttons. Poppers only. Decorated with slogans of my own invention: *Huh, Grrr!, Ceci n'est pas un baby*.

You grow out of your clothes: you leave your past behind you like a shed skin. We collect the pelts. As you grow older, we chop up the clothes, trimming body suits into vests to save money. We cut the feet out of babygros.

Sorry. Babygro™ is a tradename.

I have lost my defining style. I have begun to look like a dad. I seem to have covered the distance travelled by John Travolta

63

from *Saturday Night Fever* to the present in the space of just a few months.

I am wearing jumbo cords.

It's not an accident: all style is an ingratiation.

So who am I trying to impress?

In becoming unprepossessing we become in possession of ourselves.

I read in the local paper an advertisement for a club for the over-thirties. The advertisement reads, 'Dress Code: Make an Effort'.

coffee

To keep awake I drink more coffee. It only makes things worse.

C. W. Post, the American, the inventor of Postum, the grain-based coffee substitute, ran an ad: 'Is your yellow streak the coffee habit? Does it reduce your work time, kill your energy, push you into the big crowd of mongrels, deaden what thoroughbred blood you may have had and neutralize all your efforts to make money and fame?'

Post was a health nut. He shot himself, aged fifty-nine.

When you go to bed the work begins: tidying, preparing for tomorrow, catching up. Washing up.

You have released torrents of liquid.

The days are full of milk and piss and tears.

We drink tea and coffee till late at night.

You have made us incontinent.

colostrum

Mother's first milk – it used to be known as the 'beestings', recalling the suckling of infants by animals: Romulus and Remus; Aegisthus; Pelias.

Pelias was later cut to bits by his daughters and boiled.

Colostrum aids the evacuation of meconium and contains antibodies and proteins which protect you from bacterial infections.

It is rich and yellowy and comes mixed for the first two or three days with the milk. I imagine it like cream on a pint of gold-top.

We are at the checkout in the supermarket. You are asleep in the buggy. The man in the queue in front of me is smartly dressed. He wears glasses. He pays for his goods.

I follow him out of the supermarket. He sits on a bench directly outside and opens up his carrier bag. He takes out a half-pint carton of single cream. He peels off the foil wrapper from the top and drinks the cream. He wipes his mouth with his hand.

colours

At first, we dress you in segregated colours – all whites, all blues, all pinks. It's not until you're a little older that we begin to mix and match.

But once we begin, there's no stopping us. We wreathe you in stripes – knitted blankets of festive rainbow stripes, vests in hula-hoop blue-and-white artisan stripes, a whole range of stripy caps and hats, socks, booties (corduroy and woollen), dungarees, vests and T-shirts.

We dress you in stripy clothes because stripy clothes are happy clothes; they combine bright colours and make bold statements.

Stripes cry freedom. (The ancient Celts wore a tunic called a *crys*, which was dyed in bright colours in squares or stripes.)

But stripes also imply taming and imprisonment.

Stripes as metaphoric swaddling bands, the red and white stripes – or blue and white, or whatever – representing both wounds and bandages ('By his stripes ye are healed').

With your bald head, your barrel chest and your stripy chemise, you look a bit like Picasso, but you also look like a convict, and a little like Charlie Brown. You are cartoonish, caricatured, enframed.

There are colours we avoid. We do not dress you in black. Black is too sombre. There's time later for black. And yellow is unlucky.

(According to George Ferguson, in his book *Signs and Symbolism in Christian Art* (1954), 'Yellow is sometimes used to suggest infernal light, degradation, jealousy, treason, and deceit. Thus, the traitor Judas is frequently painted in a garment of dingy yellow. In the Middle Ages heretics were obliged to wear yellow.' In Giotto's *Betrayal and Arrest of Christ*, c. 1306, a beardless Judas wears a gold cloak not unlike that worn by boxers and wrestlers today, and indeed not unlike Buck Mulligan's ungirdled yellow dressing gown in *Ulysses*.)

Lots of red, though, for boys and girls: red shoes, red coats, red hats, red gloves, red T-shirts. Red is dynamic. It makes you stand out. And, traditionally, red is lucky, a protection against evil (a notion derived from the purple of priestly robes).

Also, it matches your eyes in the photos.

commonplaces

Commonplaces. Holes dug by generations of ants.
                                                Baudelaire

Yes, all babies look like Winston Churchill.

Yes, they do have tiny hands and feet.

No, No-One-Has-Ever-Felt-So-Deeply-Or-So-Much.

And no, there is nothing worse than having to admire other people's children.

It's impossible to see what's so great about them.

But obviously *you* are special, irreplaceable and thoroughly unique.

'It is correct,' wrote Marianne Moore, 'and unnotorious for the race to perpetuate itself.'

Marianne Moore was childless.

Was it Schopenhauer who wrote that 'the "principle of individuation" is the root of conceit'?

Maybe it was.

69

Maybe it was someone else.

Maybe it doesn't matter either way.

You know the old story about Christopher Columbus? He was mocked on his return to Spain after his first voyage to America. People said that his voyage was nothing much, that it was no big deal, that all that was necessary was to have thought of it first. Columbus asked his detractors to make an egg stand on end. None of them could. Columbus took the egg and broke one end gently and made it stand. The assembled crowd said that was an easy thing to do. Yes, said Columbus – with a twinkle in his eye – the only thing necessary was to have thought of it first.

comparisons

All comparisons are dangerous. It's absurd to make comparisons. Nabokov's publishers used to compare him to Ian Fleming and John Le Carré (when everyone knows he's more like Raymond Chandler).

It's difficult enough to see something clearly. It's almost impossible to appreciate what other people see in something.

'Look at that,' the comedian Rob Wilton is supposed to have said, watching from the wings of the Liverpool Alhambra as a Chinese acrobatic troupe went through their paces. 'All that because the buggers are too lazy to learn a comic song.'

From birth, you are charted against a notional plot-line on a graph. You are supposed to cling to this curve. We don't want you to go too far off the mark.

We want you to be average.

But there is no such thing as the average man. Someone had to invent the notion of the 'average man'. Someone did. His name was Adolphe Quetelet (1796–1874).

We compare you to other people's children. Often.

And yes, of course, you are better (so why are so many people convinced in later life that they're worse)?

(Why is it dangerous to compare? To compare is to objectify. Thus comparison diminishes your status as a subject, as a person. You become merely an example or an instance of quality: the best of a bunch, a top banana.)

No one could ever be good enough to marry our son or our daughter. I shall refuse permission.

I shall demand to know their birth weight.

confidence

I wake up to the sound of you crying. 5.30 a.m. Seagulls outside eating the rubbish.

I think: oh, shit.

I start my deep-breathing exercises.

I intone to myself: I am a happy, confident and successful parent. I am a happy, confident and successful parent. I am a happy, confident and successful parent.

I prepare for the day's vertical ascents and descents. Ladders, belays and lifelines: coffee, Radio 4, *Teletubbies*.

A climb is categorized as: Moderate, Difficult, Very Difficult, Severe, Very Severe, Hard Very Severe, and Extreme.

With babies you have to develop a head for heights.

But everyone still gets nervous.

Or let me mix my metaphors. Everyone gets seasick. And no one knows how to steer the ship. You have to learn.

All at sea, stuck up a mountain, 5.30 a.m. and in bed.

I think: I am a happy, confident and successful parent.

I try not to think: oh, shit.

Instead I try to think: OK, so you are announcing a problem.

And then I can think: I can solve it.

It's weird.

It works.

I've been watching *Oprah*.

Outside, the sky is bright.

c o n f u s i o n

Please, stop confusing me.

Previously I thought of life as a puzzle, and I was seeking the answer.

Now I have started to think of life as a jigsaw.

With a jigsaw you have to start by finding the edge pieces and then group the interior pieces into colours. Otherwise you can't do it.

You don't answer a jigsaw. You complete it. You just need patience, and a big table.

Child-care is like doing a jigsaw, obviously.

It is also like writing.

> Most writers – poets in especial – prefer having it understood that they compose by a species of fine frenzy – an ecstatic intuition – and would positively shudder at letting the public take a peep behind the scenes, at the elaborate and vacillating crudities of thought – at the true purposes seized only at the last moment – at the innumerable glimpses of idea that arrived not at the maturity of full view – at the fully matured fancies

discarded in despair as unmanageable – at the cautious selections and rejections – at the painful erasures and interpolations – in a word, at the wheels and pinions – the tackle for scene-shifting – the step-ladders and demon-traps – the cock's feathers, the red paint and the black patches, which, in ninety-nine cases out of the hundred, constitute the properties of the literary *histrio*.

Edgar Allan Poe, 'The Philosophy of Composition', 1846

Parents conceal the truths of composition.

Culture is a cover-up for confusion.

contraception

At a wedding reception. Three children: two in high-chairs, one toddling. I apologize to the single woman sitting next to me.

'It's OK,' she says, looking over the top of my balding head, eyeing up the best man on the top table, 'it's a very effective form of contraception.'

conversation

You are four months old. A friend visits. He is a good person.
He sits and talks to you while I wash the dishes and tidy up.

I'm shocked. Already I've learned to ignore you: you're family.

I'm family: you interrupt me.

cookbooks

I turn for consolation to cookbooks.

But I don't actually bother cooking anything.

I have come to the conclusion that the only good cookbook is a soup cookbook.

Kettner's Book of the Table (1877):

> Whoever writes a new book on cookery has to begin with an apology – there are so many, and most of them so bad. All contain good ideas, original or borrowed; but most of them are chaotic and overlaid with rubbish, – the wildest confusion of receipts, distinctions without differences, and endless repetitions, – the result of stupidity, of vanity, and of slavish deference to authority.

Replace the word 'cookery' here with the word 'babies'.

I don't want food I have to fiddle with. I don't even want food I have to eat with my hands.

I only want food I can drink.

couvade

Is the simulation of the experience of childbirth. The man goes to bed, is confined. It is a tradition apparently still practised by the Basques and Amazonian Indians.

I don't try it myself, but the birth does make me feel a little shaky.

crawling

At nine months you start to drag yourself along the ground, snaking around on your belly. With a full nappy, and your dirty face and cackle, it's satanic.

Within a week you are crawling on all fours, careering. Within another week you are pulling yourself up on furniture. Then standing, wobbling. Falling.

There is something shocking and sad about this change. It seems irreversible. We are no longer in control. You have asserted your right to freedom. You're flying.

'A widespread country tradition', according to *Hutchinson's Encyclopaedia of Superstitions* (1961), 'says it is very unlucky to step over a young child as it crawls about the floor. To do so stunts its growth.' Obviously.

crying

You spend a lot of time crying. It is annoying, disorientating and distressing, but not necessarily sad or saddening. It raises the temperature.

John Berger, in his book about a country doctor, *A Fortunate Man* (1967):

> There is a physical resemblance between a sobbing figure and a child. The 'bearing' of the adult falls away and his movements are limited to certain very primitive ones. The centre of the body once again seems to become the mouth: as though the mouth were simultaneously the place of pain and the only way by which consolation might be taken in. The whole body tends towards a foetal position. There are good physiological and psychological reasons for all this: but we can observe the similarity without knowing them. And why is the similarity so disturbing? Once more I believe the explanation goes further than our sense of convention or compassion. In some way the similarity, once established, is brutally denied. The sobbing man is not like a child. The child cries to protest. The man cries to himself. It may even be that by crying again like a child he somehow believes that he will regain the ability to recover like a child. Yet that is impossible.

Why don't we look in the mirror when we cry? Because we would be ashamed? We would stop crying, surely.

A friend tells me that as a child she did in fact look in the mirror when she cried: to observe her own upset.

I try an experiment: I show you a mirror when you are crying, and you stop momentarily. You turn away.

When you cry, you cry with your whole body. I touch your chest and it is heaving and vibrating. Your arms and legs wave uncontrollably.

'Let him cry it out.' 'Have a good cry, get it out of your system.' Crying at baptism was supposed to be a sign that the Devil was being driven away, a means of exorcism. We say, 'He's crying his little heart out.'

> In watching the infancy of my own children, I made another discovery – it is well known to mothers, to nurses, and also to philosophers – that the tears and lamentations of infants during the year or so when they have no other language of complaint run through a gamut that is as inexhaustible as the Cremona of Paganini. An ear but moderately learned in that language cannot be deceived as to the rate and modulus of the suffering which it indicates. A fretful or peevish cry cannot by any efforts make itself impassioned. The cry of impatience, of hunger, of irritation, of reproach, of alarm, are all different – different as a chorus of Beethoven from a chorus of Mozart. But if ever you saw an infant suffering for an hour, as sometimes the healthiest does, under some attack of the stomach, which has the tiger-grasp of the Oriental cholera, then you will hear moans that address to their mothers an anguish of supplication for aid such as might

storm the heart of Moloch. Once hearing it, you will not
forget it.

Thomas De Quincey, Suspiria de Profundis (1845)

I assume at first that you cry because you cannot speak.
Gramsci: 'The crisis consists precisely in the fact that the old is
dying and the new cannot be born; in this interregnum a great
variety of morbid symptoms appears.'

Yet when you can speak, you still cry.

Charles Darwin made a study of children crying. He wrote to
his friend Thomas Huxley:

> I rejoice that your children are all pretty well. Give Mrs
> Huxley the enclosed queries and ask her to look out when
> one of her children is struggling and just going to burst out
> crying. A dear young lady near here, plagued a very young
> child, for my sake, till it cried, and saw the eyebrows for a
> second or two beautifully oblique just before the torrent of
> tears began.

Crying is beautiful. Which is presumably why we make
ourselves and other people cry.

curtains

The curtain problem in summary: babies wake up when it's light outside.

The answer to the curtain problem in summary: buy blackout lining, blackout blinds and knock up a plyboard pelmet.

death

Birth makes you think about death, naturally.

In the Book of Common Prayer, there is a prayer, 'The Thanksgiving of Women After Child-Birth': 'The snares of death compassed me round about; and the pains of hell gat hold upon me.'

The sheer excitement of childbirth is morbid. Kafka, *Diaries* (1911):

> 10 December. Sunday. I must go to see my sister and her little boy. When my mother came home from my sister's at one o'clock at night the day before yesterday with the news of the boy's birth, my father marched through the house in his nightshirt, opened all the doors, woke me, the maid, and my sisters and proclaimed the birth as though the child had not only been born, but as though it had already lived an honourable life and been buried too.

You are a reminder to us that we're going to die. Martin Luther is said to have worn a gold finger-ring with a small death's head in enamel and the words '*Mori saepe cogita*' ('Think often of death'). Round the setting was engraved, '*O mors, ero mors tua*' ('O death, I will be thy death').

You are a living breathing memento mori.

(We discuss it. I say I don't want any fuss: just have my body laid in a porphyry sarcophagus supported by life-size marble lions. Thanks.)

Death says, 'Think.'

S. Josephine Baker, in her book Fighting for Life (1939):

> It may seem like a cold-blooded thing to say, but someone ought to point out that the World War was a backhanded break for children ... As more and more thousands of men were slaughtered every day, the belligerent nations, on whatever side, began to see that new human lives, which could grow up to replace brutally extinguished adult lives, were extremely valuable national assets ... When a nation is fighting a war or preparing for another ... it must look to its future supplies of cannon fodder.

decorating

Civilization takes a lot of paint.

Do not use gloss with a babe in arms.

A lick of paint is not to be recommended.

depression

'Are we downhearted? No!' sang Florrie Forde back in 1914.

Well, yes, actually, we are. We are downhearted. And we are washed out, often upset, peeved, annoyed, rubbed up the wrong way, tired and generally irritable.

Isn't everyone?

I think I know why. You remind us – you present to us – the meaninglessness of all our efforts. Every day it seems like starting over again. Like stacking chairs in a very large school hall.

We weave all day, but at night someone undoes the weaving. Like Penelope (the one married to Odysseus).

In Robert Crawford's Scots dialect poem 'Babby' he writes of 'bane o ma bane'. He means bone of my bone. He also means bane of my bane.

Sometimes it feels like . . . cracking my teeth on ceramic apples. Sometimes it feels like ants all over me. What is it? Am I depressed?

I read a book about a man suffering severe clinical depression.

It cheers me up.

I am not suffering severe clinical depression.

I'm a dad.

Apparently, ANTS are Automatic Negative Thoughts.

descriptions

There's no point my attempting to describe you.

The best description of a person in all of literature:

Head	Small and round
Eyes	Green
Complexion	White
Hair	Yellow
Features	Mobile
Neck	13"
Upper arm	11"
Forearm	9"

Samuel Beckett,
Murphy (1938)

That'll do.

development

We worry about your development, but your development is assured.

It's what kind of development that matters.

digestion

The process of your feeding and shitting turns white to dark.

Not immediately, of course. The time it takes breast milk to pass through the digestive tract is about fifteen hours, twenty-eight hours for formula. I imagine it slowly discolouring in the belly, darkening as it moves towards earth, the body like a conveyor belt, a door into darkness.

'What do you think bowels are?' asks the Daddy in Paul Durcan's poem 'Study of a Figure in a Landscape, 1952': 'I think bowels are wheels, Daddy, / Black wheels under my tummy, Daddy'.

This fundamental act of transformation represents a looping and doubling from front to back and top to bottom, turning the inside out and inside out again: mother's milk produced, expressed, exchanged, ingested and excreted. The movement follows a parabolic return to earth, a curving, downward process from body to body, from breast to mouth to arse. A metamorphosis. Food become dirt.

I scoff my food, and the natural processes of my own digestion are interrupted. You make me bilious.

dirt

To the pure there is nothing pure.

When you go to bed I wash my hands and face.

The lawyer Jaggers, in *Great Expectations*:

> I embrace this opportunity of remarking that he washed his
> clients off, as if he were a surgeon or a dentist. He had a
> closet in his room, fitted up for the purpose, which smelt
> of scented soap, like a perfumer's shop . . . When I and my
> friends repaired to him at six o'clock next day, he seemed
> to have been engaged on a case of a darker complexion than
> usual, for we found him with his head butted into this
> closet, not only washing his hands, but laving his face and
> gargling his throat.

I have started to floss.

When I watch television all I can think is, Jennifer Aniston is
so clean.

disappointment

I am disappointed with myself.
All dreams become nightmares.

disease

I order up from the British Library a book called *A Colour Atlas of the Newborn* (1984), by R. D. G. Milner and S. M. Herbert. I do not check the details in the catalogue. I do not know what to expect.

The book is horrific, terrifying. There are photographs of babies with gross cleft lips and huge palates like pink intestines curling out of their mouths. There are babies covered in Mongolian spots and lymphangioma, lacerations, stains. There are diseases, growths and ulcerations of unimaginable proportions.

In their preface to the book the authors write: 'In bringing the slides together we found that our colleagues with collections had, as philatelists do, a large amount of material in common and the occasional gem of their own.'

As philatelists do? The occasional gem?

Sometimes I wonder about doctors.

doctors

You bring us into contact with doctors.

Doctors do not seem to like babies. (Most doctors are men.)

I wonder, do doctors really like anything?

Medical training presumably wrings out all but the most necessary of emotions – liking is not only superfluous, it's an impediment.

I learn how to handle the doctors.

'You need a good bedside manner with doctors or you will get nowhere' – William Burroughs, Junkie (1953).

dogs

Dogs and babies do not mix.

There seem to be dogs everywhere in the parks, in the streets, nosing at you, barking at you, ready to lick you or worse.

'Don't worry,' say owners, 'they won't bite.' I shoo them away.

Ruskin had a bit of his lip bitten off by a dog and James Joyce – wasn't Joyce bitten on the chin?

There are 18 dogs and 0 cats in the Bible.

d o o r s

We are forced to rest content with assumptions – if
I want the door to turn, the hinges must stay put.
Ludwig Wittgenstein, *On Certainty*

This is a rule: you must open the door for people pushing
buggies.

Not to do so proves that civilization is descending into
barbarism. It is proof of the existence of evil.

At times, opening the door into your room in the morning is
like entering a fetid toilet: there is a fug, a heaviness in the air,
which is both appalling and enlivening ('I love the smell of
napalm in the morning,' says Robert Duvall's Colonel Kilgore
in *Apocalypse Now*). The smell is hard to shift: it lingers like
cigarette smoke.

dreams

The first months take on an illusory quality, as if watching or performing in a drama, a world existing in what Coleridge in his Notebooks called 'Somnial or Morphean Space'.

The extent to which these early months are a success depends on the extent to which this drama/dream can be rationalized. It requires both a willing suspension of disbelief and an involuntary, terrifying collapse of will.

Before you were born I started dreaming.

In my dreams you are not an adult but a baby who looks or talks like an adult, like the children in Charles Schulz's Peanuts, children who don't talk like children but who behave like children – the stuff of nightmares.

The dreams are nightmares.

I wake up and feel around for you in the bed. You are not there. I have lost you.

I go to pick you up in the morning. You are sitting looking at me. You look like Allen Ginsberg: you wear horn-rim glasses and dungarees, and have beads around your neck.

Actually, no you're not Allen Ginsberg. You're more like Peter

Sellers in his Toulouse-Lautrec disguise in *The Revenge of the Pink Panther*.

Are these dreams the fulfilment of repressed wishes? Jung:

> The view that dreams are merely the imaginary fulfilments of repressed wishes is hopelessly out of date. There are, it is true, dreams which manifestly represent wishes or fears, but what about all the other things? Dreams may contain ineluctable truths, philosophical pronouncements, illusions, wild fantasies, memories, plans, anticipations, irrational experiences, even telepathic visions . . .

There are many other, terrible dreams, too terrible to write. They seem to express the feeling that you have absorbed us, that we are dissolving into you.

Homer, in *The Odyssey*, translated by A. T. Murray, Book XIX:

> dreams verily are baffling and unclear of meaning, and in no wise do they find fulfilment in all things for men. For two are the gates of shadowy dreams, and one is fashioned of horn and one of ivory. Those dreams that pass through the gate of sawn ivory deceive men, bringing words that find no fulfilment. But those that come forth through the gate of polished horn bring true issues to pass, when any mortal sees them.

We discuss dreams. I wonder what they mean.

'They mean cut out the coffee and cheese.'

dribble

How long wilt thou not depart from me, nor let me
alone till I swallow down my spittle?

Job 7:19

Like soup noodles. So loquacious.

Your damp clothes: their slight caramel sweetness, slightly
herby, a little loamy. Like something living.

The high-tide marks: the eddies and currents of you.

driving

After we bought the car we had to buy a car seat. And then a bigger car seat. Then, finally, a booster seat.

It's difficult to persuade our parents of the importance of strapping you in correctly: they merely wave the seat-belt vaguely in your direction.

My mum says, we just used to sit you on the back in your cot.

I say, I really don't think it's a good idea while driving to sit babies on the back seat in a cot, or even on a passenger's lap. Nor is it a good idea to carry sharp wood, or metal, to attempt to administer wet food, breast-feed, or to answer calls. Nor should one wear hatpins with unprotected points. Or engage in rough play.

'It's all this political correctness,' says my dad.

But we draw the line at a sign saying 'Baby on Board'. We're not asking for special treatment.

drugs

We visit a friend, an American. She is taking her children to visit her family in the States. How will she manage on the flight with her two lively young boys, we ask. 'Drug 'em,' she says. We're shocked.

Is this an American thing?

Actually, babies throughout the ages and in many cultures have been fed drugs to keep them quiet.

Wet nurses smeared their nipples with laudanum.

My parents fed me whisky.

And opium was for a long time the preferred drug of choice for both adults and children in England, retailed for babies in the form of Atkinson's Infants' Preservative, Godfrey's Cordial ('The Comfort'), Mrs Winslow's Soothing Syrup and Street's Infants' Quietness.

Thomas De Quincey called opium 'Divine Poppy-juice, as indispensable as breathing'.

I try the gas and air in the hospital. It's like being drunk on air. I feel like Emily Dickinson.

And the feeling seems never to have left me.

You're like drugs. Not the head-in-the-clouds-reclining-on-a-cushion-sucking-on-a-hookah kind of drug experience, but that parched and jaw-slackening heaviness that comes from late-night drinking.

What's the word I'm looking for?

Lassitude (a good name for a baby – you could call it Lassie for short).

We try to do without stimulants: breast-feeding mothers aren't supposed to drink. I come out in support.

But who can do without stimulants and comforts? Bonaparte relied on snuff, Byron on gin-and-water, Newton on tobacco, and Pope on coffee. I know a lot of Christians who eat a lot of biscuits.

You get a lot of fat people in churches.

I eat so many biscuits and drink so much coffee it makes me feel sick.

Someone I haven't seen for a long time asks me, 'Well, what have you been doing, apart from the baby?' All I can answer is that I've been drinking a lot of coffee. 'No, really,' they say. But it's true. That's what I've been doing.

dungarees

Dungarees are work-clothes suitable for adults: they are simple, hard-wearing and unpretentious; they have pockets strategically placed for tools and pencils and pieces of paper.

For babies under about six months dungarees are totally impractical: they are a pose.

A four-month-old baby does not need the pouches and pockets for chisels or claw-hammers, and in the summer the thick material leaves you too hot, with sweat forming under the straps and across the chest, and in the winter too cool, requiring a jumper or a coat to cover your arms.

I buy a poacher's waistcoat, with plenty of pockets for bottles and rice cakes and tiny boxes of raisins.

I do not look like a poacher.

I look like a paramilitary.

No, not even that good.

I look like the Unabomber.

But I can't get away with a handbag.

e a r s

I like the way your ears join your head, the fact that it's impossible to see the join. I like the way your ears are cool to the touch.

I like everything about you. In the 1937 film *Shall We Dance?* Fred Astaire sings to Ginger Rogers:

> The way you wear your hat,
> the way you sip your tea,
> the mem'ry of all that –
> No, no! They can't take that away from me!

I learn a new phrase, the 'auricular point', the point at the top of the orifice of the ear.

What if you turn out ugly? What if your ears get too big?

S. J. Perelman, in 'Mid-Winter Facial Trends': 'Personally, I have found that a short length of three-quarter-inch manila hemp bound stoutly about the head, the knot protruding just below one's hat, adds a rakish twist to the features and effectively prisons ears inclined to flap in the wind . . .'

My mother tried it with me, apparently. Or not.

eating

Parents do not eat: they feed. A. J. Liebling:

> I use the verb 'to eat' here to denote a selective activity, as
> opposed to the passive acceptance and regular renewal of
> nourishment, learned in infancy. An automobile receiving
> fuel at a filling station or an infant at the breast cannot be
> said to eat, nor can a number of people at any time in their
> lives.

Six months in, I go out with a friend. We drink a good bottle
of wine and eat a dozen oysters. I can't really afford it. I
recommend it.

education

A friend with older children says, 'I've learned a lot from my children.' I think maybe she's putting it on.

But I'm not ashamed to admit it. I've learned some lessons.

More difficult than learning a foreign language. More difficult than French or German. More than a new vocabulary and a grammar.

You've taught me – I don't know what – and you can't even speak. There's a lesson there.

Frank O'Hara in his poem 'Hotel Particulier': 'I had a teacher one whole summer who never told me / anything and it was wonderful.'

emotions

We become drunk on emotion: the drama; the events; the momentum; the trials and tribulations. It's refreshing, like a cold beer on a hot day in a foreign country.

I begin to recognize patterns of emotions: dread and depression early in the morning; exhaustion around lunchtime; elation towards 7. These patterns happen to correspond with your waking and sleeping times.

A distant relative tells me about another even more distant relative: 'For an alcoholic he has high standards. He doesn't start drinking till 5.' I resolve to do the same.

encouragement

Success with your children. Two words: 'Attaboy!', 'Attagirl!'

entertainment

All parents are children's entertainers – plate-spinners, equipose artists. We're all Risley acts.

(Professor Risley was a music-hall performer who juggled children with his feet. The legend goes that he committed suicide after the death of a child in the act. In fact, he died in a lunatic asylum.)

Personally, I specialize in shadowography and paper-tearing.

epidural

After the birth, I look up anaesthetic in *Black's Medical Dictionary*. My eye is drawn to the description of stage IV of anaesthesia:

> This is the stage of danger, the breathing becomes shallow, the face pallid or livid, the heart weak and irregular, and the pupils widely dilated. If the anaesthetic be not at once removed, breathing and pulse then stop and the person dies.

Queen Victoria, pregnant with her eighth child, was administered chloroform (first introduced in 1847). Some theologians objected: they thought pain in childbirth was what God intended. The first mother to receive chloroform in labour called her baby Anaesthesia.

'Did it hurt?' I ask.

'What do you think?'

expectations

It's true what people say. You can't have everything. You are a lesson in the principle of opportunity cost.

We expect anything and everything. We expect the contradictory and the impossible. We expect compact cars which are spacious; luxurious cars which are economical. We expect to be rich and charitable, powerful and merciful, active and reflective, kind and competitive. We expect to be inspired by mediocre appeals for 'excellence', to be made literate by illiterate appeals for literacy. We expect to eat and stay thin, to be constantly on the move and ever more neighbourly, to go to the 'church of our choice' and yet feel its guiding power over us, to revere God and to be God.

Never have people been more the masters of their environment. Yet never has a people felt more deceived and disappointed. For never has a people expected so much more than the world could offer.

Daniel Boorstin, *The Image* (1961)

experience

I can't decide. Are you broadening my horizons or obscuring the view?

'A man who has climbed the Matterhorn may prefer Derbyshire to Switzerland, but he won't think the Peak is the highest mountain in Europe' – Ezra Pound, *ABC of Reading* (1934).

You're not what I expected.

I don't know what I expected.

Actually, I expected nothing.

Was it Freud who said, 'Experience consists in experiencing what we do not wish to experience'? Or was it Woody Allen?

We're bickering. I'm complaining.

'I have never touched a diamond,' I say.

'Nor have you ever kissed a leper.'
Good point, well made.

e y e s

Sometimes you open your eyes so wide we can see the whole round iris. We can see the curvature of the eyeball, the small bulge, the cornea. I stare into your eyes. I stare at your eyes. But I cannot hold your gaze for very long. You disconcert me.

Giacometti, in an interview: 'The eye is something special in so far as it's almost as though made of a different material from the rest of the face.'

At first you stare vacantly, then at about four weeks you start to stare at sounds.

At about four months your head becomes suddenly more mobile. You have the head of a robot, swivelling around.

I'm half expecting 360°.

eyebrows

You have pencil-thin eyebrows, like Marlene Dietrich, and my nan.

face

Your baby face is fleshy – featureless. It looks indolent, relaxed, happy. The only other face I have seen look anything like it is the face of my grandfather, in his coffin.

As you grow older the facial expressions become more complex; it's almost as if the skin is being pulled tighter and tighter over a face that pre-exists beneath, or as if the head is still moulding itself into shape.

It is quite possible to believe, like Ruskin, that the faces of people become daily more corrupt: Tony Blair puffing up into a US president – the face and the shape of responsibility.

From the day you were born, your face is a parade of expressions. Yet there's so much you can't do. You don't blush, or flush. You don't raise your eyebrows. You don't wink. You have a face, but there is no façade. You laugh uncontrollably and cry uncontrollably. You do not attend to yourself. Therefore you are totally vulnerable: your face has no disguise, there is no dissembling.

In your face, other faces appear: the face of my grandfather, who died before you were born, my father, my mother, my father-in-law, my mother-in-law, sisters, brothers, aunts, uncles, people I have never even met, people whose faces exist only in old photos.

You communicate by expression. You make us laugh. You make us cry. Your face is a work of art. ('The function of the arts,' writes the poet Derek Mahon, 'is not to change maps but to change the expressions on the faces of men and women.')

We stare at your face as if it might reveal some tremendous secret. It is another form of divination: necromancy, pyromancy, oenomancy, neomancy, pedomancy, hydromancy, geomancy, physiognomy, chiromancy, metoposcopy.

Johann Caspar Lavater published his first treatise 'On Physiognomy' in 1772. In 1778 he published his four-volume study, which was translated by Henry Hunter and appeared in five volumes in English between 1789 and 1798, titled *Essays on Physiognomy, Designed to Promote the Knowledge and Love of Mankind*.

Lavater's definition of physiognomy:

> By Physiognomy then I mean, the talent of discovering the interior of Man by his exterior – of perceiving by certain natural signs, what does not immediately strike the senses . . . Physiognomy would accordingly be, the Science of discovering the relation between the exterior and the interior – between the visible surface and the invisible spirit which it covers – between the animated, perceptible matter, and the imperceptible principle which impresses this character of life upon it – between the apparent effect, and the concealed cause which produces it.

Lavater is no better than Freud, or no worse.

families

Families in the shopping mall on a Saturday afternoon, buggies like prows cleaving the waves. I imagine huge Busby Berkeley dance routines.

Sometimes I think, it's like we are related, and then I realize, we *are* related.

Someone says to me, apropos of nothing in particular, if you go back 650 years you'll have 114 million relatives.

You are six months old. I am reading a book about the Jonestown mass suicide. It occurs to me that families have all the characteristics of a cult: élitism, secrecy, personality cults, ego destruction, rules of obedience. That afternoon we're on the bus. You're in the buggy. I overhear this conversation:

> 'I mean, we were close. Not incest or anything, but really really close. You know, like we knew what each other were thinking. He said to me once, you know, I wish we weren't cousins, so we could get married. And anyway, this big fight we had and he gets this knife and says, "I'm going to kill you." Now, I've got a good sense of humour and everything, but that's just not funny, is it?'

I find myself saying strange things to you like, 'Let's run away and get married.'

There's something odd about families. There's something sad about families.

There is something so sad about families it makes us rush to form other families.

Joyce in *Finnegans Wake* (1939), Anna Livia Plurabella remembering her father: 'And it's old and old it's sad and old it's sad and weary I go back to you, my cold father, my cold mad father, my cold mad feary father, till the near sight of the mere size of him, the moyles and moyles of it, moananoaning, makes me seasilt saltsick and I rush, my only, into your arms.'

fat

As you grow your body becomes fat. At first, your limbs are thin. Then they are fat, like huge sausages. A butcher's, plain pork.

Eventually, at about six months, your limbs are too fat even to be described as sausages. It's as if padding has been inserted under the skin. You look stuffed. You look quilted and puffy. Like the strange intestinal folds of fat illustrated in Leonardo da Vinci's studies of a baby (c. 1478). Or like Beryl Cook's roly-polies – the fat barely contained, the bodies compressed and simplified.

We call you 'sausage'.

I can't believe I'm calling anyone sausage. All those years of education . . .

But you are like a pig.

In their book The Symbolic Pig: An anthology of Pigs in Literature and Art (1961), Frederick Cameron Sillar and Ruth Mary Meyler claim that 'Babies and pigs have always seemed to have something in common.' But they don't say what.

Pigs and babies are clumsy, dirty, gluttonous, and they move around on all fours.

G. K. Chesterton:

> The actual lines of a pig (I mean a really fat pig) are about the loveliest and most luxuriant in nature; the pig has the same great curves, swift and yet heavy, which we see in rushing water or in rolling cloud . . . There is no point of view from which a really corpulent pig is not full of sumptuous and satisfying curves . . . he has that fuller, subtler, and more universal kind of shapeliness which the unthinking (gazing at pigs and distinguished journalists) mistake for a mere absence of shape.

You look like Leigh Bowery, Lucian Freud's (dead) fat Australian model.

No, of course you don't look like Leigh Bowery.

Leigh Bowery looked like a baby.

Probably God looks like a baby.

What I mean is, God is an endomorph. (Which makes Jesus an ectomorph and the Holy Ghost a mesomorph.)

My parents buy half a pig, already butchered and bagged – chops, sausages, bacon, shanks, etc. – from a man who advertises in the local paper. It costs £50. They are very pleased with it. My mum calls it a pig bag. It lasts them nearly six months.

I ask, 'Is it all from the same pig?'

And my mum says, of course it's all from the same pig.

I say, 'How do you know?'

No reply.

I say, 'A whole half?'

'What do you mean?'

'All the bits?'

'Yes.'

Everything in a pig is good.

fathers

Mothers need fathers more than babies need fathers. It's a biological fact.

Nearly everything I read about fathers is untrue: it's all mocked up. It's a performance.

When I read something true about fathers I write it down.

Three examples.

First, Bertrand Russell, in his *Autobiography* (1967–69):

> Parental feeling, as I have experienced it, is very complex. There is, first and foremost, sheer animal affection, and delight in watching what is charming in the ways of the young. Next, there is the sense of inescapable responsibility, providing a purpose for daily activities which scepticism does not easily question. Then there is an egoistic element, which is very dangerous: the hope that one's children may succeed where one has failed, that they may carry on one's work when death or senility puts an end to one's own efforts, and, in any case, that they will supply a biological escape from death, making one's own life part of the whole stream, and not a mere stagnant puddle without any overflow into the future. All this I

experienced, and for some years it filled my life with happiness and peace.

Second, Katherine Tait, in *My Father Bertrand Russell* (1975):

He played at being a father . . . and he acted the part to perfection, but his heart was elsewhere and his combination of inner detachment and outer affection caused me much muddled suffering.

And Anton Chekhov, in a letter translated by Constance Garnett:

Noah had three sons, Shem, Ham, and Japheth. Ham only noticed that his father was a drunkard, and completely lost sight of the fact that he was a genius, that he had built an ark and saved the world.

I can find almost nothing more positive, from 2,000 years of Western culture.

So we can't just blame Homer Simpson.

fear

No one will you tell you this, but it's true. You will wake up
in the middle of the night. Your baby will be sleeping. You
will kneel down next to the cot to check that they are
breathing.

The surge of love we feel for you is akin to fear. There is an
excess of feeling that exhausts and motivates.

There is the fear of what might become of you in the future.

We decide not to fear this. We take out life insurance. We
make a will. The language of assertion, the last gasp: I APPOINT, I
GIVE DEVISE AND BEQUEATH, I DIRECT, I DECLARE.

There are other sorts of fear. Sometimes we are scared, not
exactly scared of you, but almost. The fear is not knowing
what you might do next. Sometimes you like to be held tight,
other times you don't. It's not really scary. It's just
complicated.

But complications can be scary: take love, for example.

At seven months, I go into your room in the morning. You are
awake and on all fours. You look up at me, as if I've disturbed
you. It scares the life out of me. You've turned into something
else.

I need a brandy.

There is a Charles Addams cartoon in which husband and wife are going out for the evening, leaving the two children with a baby-sitter: "We won't be late, Miss Weems. Get the children to bed around eight, and keep your back to the wall at all times.'

feeding

In America I see a man eating a whole fried chicken, with potatoes, from a paper plate, walking along in a food hall in a mall. He is totally self-absorbed.

Just off the A40, a month later, early one morning, three yellow-fluorescent-jacketed street-sweepers are standing by the side of the road. Barrow and brooms laid aside, they are bending forwards. I look closer. They are eating blackberries, oblivious.

You suck your hands, devouring yourself.

'Our delight in food is rooted in our immense relish at the thought that, prospectively, we are eating ourselves' – J. G. Ballard.

Boswell describes Johnson eating:

> When at table, he was totally absorbed in the business of the moment; his looks seemed riveted to his plate; nor would he, unless when in very high company, say one word, or even pay the least attention to what was said by others, till he had satisfied his appetite, which was so fierce, and indulged with such intenseness, that while in the act of eating, the veins of his forehead swelled, and generally a strong perspiration was visible.

From the very first, your eating is frantic. You gorge, and then fall into a stupor. It's a terrifying sight, obscene, like Rubens's *Drunken Silenus*, with the satyress suckling the twin *panismi*, fondling the penis of one of them, milk leaking across their cheeks. The sight of you feeding reminds me of Coleridge's 'Kubla Khan':

> Weave a circle round him thrice,
> And close your eyes with holy dread,
> For he on honey dew hath fed
> And drunk the milk of Paradise.

We eat a lot of tinned ravioli.

I long for roast crown of lamb with stuffing, apple and mint jelly, and new potatoes. I long for three-course meals and puddings, meals I have never eaten. I long for roast pigeon on a smooth mash with braised leeks and truffle butter. I long for a leisurely breakfast of devilled kidneys and the papers. One night I even dream a menu. It consists of watercress soup, poached salmon with a cream sauce, and Paris-Brest, with lemonade to drink.

But what to feed you?

I'm running out of time and ideas.

I consider cooking up steak and kidney pie in a two-gallon bucket, waiting until there's a good golden bloom upon its crust, then throwing it into a pail with boiling potatoes and fresh peas, liquidizing the lot and freezing it into tiny cubes. I could make it up once a week. We'd have to buy a big chest-freezer and keep it in the hall. But you'd be happy, and I could just drink my meals.

feelings

For the first six months, you feel sensations. You do not perceive. You know only yourself.

You cannot feel embarrassment. You don't care how you look in other people's eyes. Nothing is hidden. You are not incompetent, or inexperienced, or ignorant. There is no blushing or dithering. You are not shy.

Another pseudo-science popular among parents, like phrenology, physiognomy, and Freudian psychology: pathognomy (the interpretation of emotions by observing facial or bodily expressions).

We try this also.

It doesn't work.

fontanelles

The fontanelles, the soft spots, literally the 'little fountains'.

There are six of them. Two big ones – front of head and back.

A friend, a scientist, tells me that the brain is mostly water and weighs no more than a can of Coke. I imagine inside your head the contents of a miniature can of Coke.

'My mind is troubled like a fountain stirred, and I myself see not the bottom of it' – *Troilus and Cressida*, Act 3, Scene 3.

I imagine your insides: fontanelle, skin, muscle, skull, membrane. All the little passageways and tunnels. I look into your ear, and imagine your tiny brain.

I remember that scene in Iain Banks's novel *The Wasp Factory* (1984), pp. 139–142 in the Abacus paperback edition. Underlined in my own copy, unannotated, too shocking even for an exclamation mark.

I try not to remember it.

I remember instead that fontanella is a sparkling wine made in New Zealand.

But that's no better: I imagine a fountain of wine springing up from within you. Or Coke.

forgetting

You are three months old. I go out with you in the buggy. I see three interesting things.

One: an old woman wearing a woolly hat like a pork-pie crust lying under a tartan blanket on the Holloway Road, attended by a paramedic wearing biker boots.

Two: a middle-aged woman on the 253 bus popping chocolates into her mouth, holding and then sucking the chocolates in her cheek, like a chipmunk.

And already I can't remember the third.

Coleridge: 'At what time were we dipped in the Lethe, which has thus produced such utter oblivion of a state so godlike?'

How and when do we lose ourselves?

friends

Qui me amat, amat et canem meam: love me, love my dog.

Do our friends have to like you? No, of course not. We choose friends for different reasons, for other qualities.

But are they still our friends if they don't like you? No, of course not.

Most of our friends seem scared of you. They don't know what to do with you. They don't really want to be with you: you are not their friend. I feel the same about other people's babies.

We make new friends. Our new friends also have children. But we have almost nothing else in common with them. It's like the army. When we move we lose contact.

Even our best friends don't come round much any more. When we invite them they stay for shorter periods. This is both a good and a bad thing. A necessity and an excuse. We are tired. They are appalled.

We offer you to them to hold, as we might offer a cup of coffee. 'Do you want to hold him?' 'Tea or coffee?' Sometimes we slip up and forget. 'I can't remember if you take sugar or not.'

A friend says, 'No no no!' when we offer you to her. She says she wants to admire from afar. I don't blame her. She is wearing the kind of clothes that women wear in Sunday supplements.

Germaine Greer, in *Sex and Destiny* (1984), argues that 'the modern Western infant is wanted by fewer people than any infants in our long history — not only by fewer parents, but by smaller groups of people'.

future

Sometimes it is easier to think about your future than to deal with the present.

'Distant objects please, because, in the first place, they imply an idea of space and magnitude, and because, not being obtruded too close upon the eye, we clothe them with the indistinct and airy colours of fancy' – Hazlitt, 'Why Distant Objects Please'.

One night – you're eight months old – I'm drunk and I describe you to friends as like a letter tied with ribbons in a trunk in the attic, as a message in a bottle, as a loveheart carved on a tree, an indelible marker on a municipal park bench – what we write on you, I say, will be read by others in years to come. The friends nod politely. They're drunk also.

The next morning, in Belfast, a gable-end mural is being painted over.

gardens

The gravel gardens of the rich. The concrete yards of the poor.
We want grass.

genitals

Freud, in *Civilization and Its Discontents* (1930): 'It is worth remarking that the genitals themselves, the sight of which is always exciting, are nevertheless hardly ever judged to be beautiful; the quality of beauty seems, instead, to attach to certain secondary sexual characteristics.'

Wrong again. The genitals are sublime.

Girl, your genitals are pure Georgia O'Keeffe, except smoother.

And boy, even your testes are beautiful. Like a savoy cabbage: a tiny savoy cabbage stuffed with mince. Your penis looks skinned. And your scrotum is a barometer.

Changing nappies, I think of the world's two great eunuchs: Origen (self-inflicted) and Abelard (punishment).

And of course Ts'ai Lun, who invented paper in AD 105 – he was a eunuch. And then I remember: writing is just an extension of one's power to charm.

girl

We are at a wedding. A record comes on, all the women go down on to the dance floor and begin to move in time. They put their arms in front, touch their heads, touch their waists, bend forward, shake their behinds, clap and turn and begin again.

I sit and watch with my dad, silent, drinking bitter.

grandparents

My grandparents might never have lived at all. They made no mark in the world. They were not famous. They were not rich. We gave away their clothes when they died. Kept only a few ornaments and some kitchenware – a broken clock, some saucepans, one good sharp knife, two pudding bowls.

Their children and grandchildren are the only evidence that they ever existed.

And of course you are now the evidence that I am here.

In my eyes you have transformed my parents into their parents.

And presumably in their eyes I have now become like them.

It's like Musical Chairs. We're all swapping places.

And when the music stops . . .

growth

Notches on the door-post, not ours.

When does a pebble become a stone?

When does the stone become a rock?

h a i r

No animals other than mammals have hair, and all mammals have hair (except whales). Even elephants have hair around the tail. I wonder, when does hair become fur, and fur become bristles and wool?

You start off furry and become fuzzy.

You are bald, but your head does not glisten, like my dad's: it glows.

The fuzz of hair and the glow are like a halo. You look – and I will say this only once – like an angel.

You are six months old. I take you to the barber with me – you sit in the buggy sucking your hands. The barber tells me he is leaving to become a professional kick-boxer. He demonstrates some moves. The hair is falling all around our feet.

> Babies haven't any hair;
> Old men's heads are just as bare; –
> Between the cradle and the grave
> Lies a haircut and a shave.
> Samuel Hoffenstein

I try but I cannot count the hairs on your head.

I check in a book: you should have between 129,000 and 150,000.

Who counted?

hands

You are nine months old. We are on the train. A woman on the train has a plastic hand. She's young – early twenties. The uniformity of the colour of the hand is startling: dull and pinkish, like a tongue. Her other hand is normal.

I look at your hands.

You were born with hard, flat horny finger and toenails, the roots buried in your skin. I examine your fingers, amazed by the tiny oval pattern of ridges and terminals, the whorls, the enclosures. The patterns are unique.

Your fingernails are growing. The *in vitro* nails are marked by a white line across the top. We snip them off with little scissors, like a toy. We perform a manicure. You smile up at us. The tiny clippings we throw on the floor.

As soon as you can crawl you start digging in the dirt.

We get off the train – the woman with the red hand has been smiling at you. You have been smiling back. She waves as she gets off. I pick up your hand and make you wave.

Quintilian, *Institutio Oratoria*, XI, 3:

other portions of the body merely help the speaker, whereas the hands may almost be said to speak. Do we not use them to demand, promise, summon, dismiss, threaten, supplicate, express aversion or fear, question or deny? Do we not use them to indicate joy, sorrow, hesitation, confession, penitence, measure, quantity, number and time? Have they not the power to excite and prohibit, to express approval, wonder or shame? Do they not take the place of adverbs and pronouns when we point at places and things? In fact, though the people and nations of the earth speak in a multitude of tongues, they share in common the universal language of the hands.

hate

People hate babies. Even people with babies hate babies. Especially people with babies.

I hate babies.

Hardly anyone admits to it, of course. W. C. Fields.

R. D. Laing *The Politics of Experience and the Bird of Paradise* (1967):

> From the moment of birth, when the Stone Age baby confronts the twentieth-century mother, the baby is subjected to these forces of violence, called love, as its father and mother and their parents and their parents before them, have been. These forces are mainly concerned with destroying most of its potential.

I am surprised at my own emotional responses. They are so limited. I enjoy none of the emotions I read about in books, not even in R. D. Laing. Especially not R. D. Laing. I usually feel only a mild fascination (bathing you, playing with you), some indifference (feeding you absent-mindedly) and, occasionally, anger (why won't you fucking shut up/feed/sleep?).

But then again, and on the other hand, with a little effort I can work myself up to anything.

George Orwell, in a review of *The Totalitarian Enemy* by F. Borkenau, in *Time and Tide*, 4 May 1940:

> As for the hate-campaigns in which totalitarian régimes ceaselessly indulge, they are real enough while they last, but are simply dictated by needs of the moment. Jews, Poles, Trotskyists, English, French, Czechs, Democrats, Fascists, Marxists — almost anyone can figure as Public Enemy No. 1. Hatred can be turned in any direction at a moment's notice, like a plumber's blow-flame.

We're standing in a queue. A woman with four children, all under five: a boy, two girls and a baby. The eldest, the boy, pushes the youngest, a girl. The girl falls over and starts crying. The woman slaps the boy around the head. 'Behave!' she screams at the boy. 'Get up!' she yells at the girl. The girl does not get up. 'Get up, you wee bitch!' The girl gets up. The baby starts to howl. 'Shut up!' howls the woman. I check my watch. It is 8.45 a.m.

headaches

We share a constant, gentle little headache.

home

The flat doesn't feel like home any more.

It's like we've been colonized, taken over. It's like we've moved out, or gone underground. Or Underground: it's like we're surviving on slot-machine chocolate, going round and round on the Circle Line.

Having a baby is like deciding to leave home and go to live in another country. You give up your job, pack up and sell up, set out for your destination, and at first it's like being on holiday: you take long walks and lots of photos, and it's fun.

But eventually you get bored and you begin to lose touch with the people you used to know back home, you begin to run out of money, and you can't understand why you ever came here in the first place. But it's too late. You're stranded. You stand out. You're an expat.

No. That's not right. Having a baby is not like visiting another country. Having a baby is more like being locked into a cell. Or your own home. Except the phone doesn't ring any more. And the postman brings only bills.

For the first time in our lives we are thinking about having our milk delivered. We're not going anywhere.

humour

Everything is funny as long as it is happening to someone else: the non-sleepers and non-eaters; the baby that vomits all over her mother's meal in a fancy restaurant; the baby left in its car seat on the roof of a car while the parents drive off; the baby who eats only Marmite on toast and shits only twice a week.

You make me laugh so much I have to wipe my eyes with toilet-roll paper.

We have started buying Kleenex.

innocence

There is nothing innocuous left. The little pleasures,
expressions of life that seemed exempt from the
responsibility of thought, not only have an element of
defiant silliness, of callous refusal to see, but directly serve
their diametrical opposite. Even the blossoming tree lies the
moment its bloom is seen without the shadow of terror;
even the innocent 'How lovely!' becomes an excuse for an
existence outrageously unlovely, and there is no longer
beauty or consolation except in the gaze falling on horror,
withstanding it, and in unalleviated consciousness of
negativity holding fast to the possibility of what is better . . .
Among today's adept practitioners, the lie has long since lost
its honest function of misrepresenting reality. Nobody
believes anybody, everyone is in the know. Lies are told
only to convey to someone that one has no need either of
him or his good opinion. The lie, once a liberal means of
communication, has today become one of the techniques of
insolence enabling each individual to spread around him the
glacial atmosphere in whose shelter he can thrive.

Theodor Adorno, *Minima Moralia*,
trans. E. F. N. Jephcott (1978)

inside

You have come from the inside of one body – tucked away down below the heart, alongside the intestine, the lungs and bladder – and now you are on the outside. You have become a living surface. We cannot see your interior, and you cannot express it.

When you were born you were covered in goo and gloop – the murky stuff of inside. Is this why when we imagine aliens they are slimy and dark, because they are from our hidden depths?

In *Inhibitions, Symptoms and Anxiety* (1926), Freud writes that 'there is more continuity between intra-uterine life and earliest infancy than the impressive caesura of the act of birth would have us believe'.

You are still gestating.

interpreting

I am at a party, a few of us are watching a Bollywood film.

Someone has to explain to me what is happening. It's not just that I can't understand the language. I don't appreciate the conventions. Subtitles or dubbing would make no difference. The whole makes no sense.

'All human knowledge takes the form of interpretation', according to Walter Benjamin.

The first year of your life is a challenge to interpretation: we are constantly trying to interpret your behaviour. We are given to understand that your crying is a signal, a sign, rather than simply an exercise or a gratuitous act of will. Everything explains everything else. We are constantly searching for meanings and clues. We go off on tangents. We concoct. We become co-conspirators.

It's like cops and robbers.

The Cop With The Theory No One Believes In.

The Inscrutable Villain.

We're no better than thieves and blackmailers: we extort from you.

Parents deal in small-change Freudianisms and vulgar ultra-Darwinisms.

invisibility

We are exposed.

We are invisible.

In Wales, years ago, up a mountain. And far below, a couple having a conversation on the road could be clearly heard.

irony

Babies do not appreciate irony, or religion.

Life with a baby becomes more melodramatic, more full of pathos. It's like living in America. Actually, Americans are very good with babies.

You do not appreciate irony, but you are an irony.

> An antipoetic posture grows out of the conviction that between what we think about ourselves and what we actually are there exists an infinite distance, just as there is an infinite distance between what we wish things were and what they are, or between what we think they are and what they are. To apprehend this distance, this abyss, means to destroy the poetic illusion. This is also the essence of the art of irony. And irony is the perspective of the novel.
>
> Milan Kundera, *Life is Elsewhere* (1986)

I find myself becoming increasingly sincere. I find myself becoming a victim of my own genuine feelings.

jars

Food in jars is all the same colour as baked beans and has the same consistency as a tin of Heinz tomato soup before it is stirred.

We become accustomed to monochrome meals.

I would prefer lobsters and strawberries.

You have diarrhoea so bad it is running down your legs. I take a sample to the doctor, in an empty jar (Baby Organix Spinach and Potato).

(The actual shit is the colour of Hippo Organic Banana and Peach Dessert.)

In 1995 the Food Commission examined the contents of 400 different products and concluded that 70 per cent were bulked out with low-nutrient starches.

Apparently, manufacturers routinely add fat and oil to their products.

The Commission concluded that the regulations governing the manufacturing of baby foods are 'lax' and misdescription is 'rife'.

Lax and Rife Baby Foods.

According to a report in the *Daily Telegraph* on 14 June 1997: 'A product calling itself premium-steak dinner . . . may consist of 10 per cent beef carcass off-cuts, 4 per cent starch thickeners, 80 per cent water, 5 per cent cooking fats and 1 per cent flavour-boosting ingredients.'

jaundice

At the end of the first week you go yellow. The liver can't cope with breaking down the foetal haemoglobin, and the bilirubin is starting to build up. That's the technical description.

It's only jaundice. It's common.

You look a little sunburned – it's like a Barbados suntan, like Bob Monkhouse's, or Frank Sinatra's.

(Coco Chanel invented the suntan. In 1922. It's not natural.)

It soon passes, and you are pale again. There's time to tan.

My parents, in retirement, out in the garden, as shiny as their brass door-knocker.

j o y

'I have no name:
I am but two days old.'
What shall I call thee?
'I happy am,
Joy is my name.'
Sweet joy befall thee!
                    William Blake,
                        'Infant Joy'

You are a joy, which is a shock.

Joy is not an emotion with which I am much familiar. With
which no one is much familiar, surely. You can have too much
of a good thing. At the very most we are accustomed to a state
of what e. e. cummings called 'nonunhappiness'.

You make me realize the unreality of despair. I wish I could
have worked this out sooner. I can't be bothered with being
miserable. Not at the moment. Maybe again when I'm
older.

Lots of writers write books out of grief: it was only after his
mother died that Proust began *A la recherche du temps perdu*.

No one writes out of happiness (except, notes a friend, Emerson, Whitman, Frank O'Hara, and Paul Weller, 'when he was with D. C. Lee').

And no one writes when they're tired. This is why there are virtually no good books about babies. Or shiftwork.

To quote Pope Leo X, 'God has given us the papacy; let us enjoy it.'

k i n d n e s s

We are relying on people's goodwill. It is not always
forthcoming.

> It is not from the benevolence of the butcher, the brewer,
> or the baker that we expect our dinner, but from their
> regard to their own interest. We address ourselves, not to
> their humanity but to their self-love, and never talk to them
> of our own necessities but of their advantages.
>> Adam Smith, *The Wealth of Nations* (1776)

Sometimes a smile would do. I am buying your fucking bread,
after all.

kisses

Your tongue and lips are wet, dark pink, liverish.

Sometimes they look scary (Sylvia Plath: 'Liver, liver / Makes me shiver'). Your mouth is shiny and raw, internal, like organ meat, or offal. The thin skin of the lips. The mucous membrane of the inside of the mouth.

Your tongue vibrates, up and down and side to side and back and forward, as if pulsing with electrical current.

Sucking, swallowing, rooting: apparently we use the same reflexes for kissing as for suckling. According to Adrianne Blue, in her book *On Kissing: From the Metaphysical to the Erotic* (1996): 'Erotic kissing is mock-suckling. Kissing is mock-feeding of the other, too: it is offering the soft, vulnerable bits of oneself, the lips, the tongue, between the other's teeth, and knowing they are safe.'

A man and woman are sitting side by side on the train. We are sitting opposite.

I somehow know the man and woman have spent the night together but that they are not 'together'. I wonder how I know this. The man sits staring forward, the woman sits leaning over slightly towards him, her legs crossed, one leg

resting against his. He asks her what she is doing at the weekend. She is going out with her friend Angie, who is 'not your average thirty-five-year-old'. They're going roller-blading. She points to a tiny bruise on her leg – 'That's not from roller-blading,' she says. They both laugh. She kisses him when she gets off – but he remains still, emotionless, facing forwards, and turns his head slightly away. He does not want to be kissed.

From the moment you are born people kiss you, and you become a hostage to kissing. 'Any Time's Kissing Time', according to the old music-hall song.

> My baby has a mottled fist,
> My baby has a neck in creases;
> My baby kisses and is kissed,
> For he's the very thing for kisses.
> Christina Rossetti

When I meet people for the first time, I shake their hand. With many of my male friends when I meet them, after years of knowing each other, we still shake hands. With some, I don't even do that. One of my closest friends I don't think I have ever touched. Nor ever will. Or would want to.

Would it be different if we were, say, Italian? Or American? Would the world be a better place if everyone were huggers?

I cannot shake your hand. You grip my finger, but I cannot reciprocate, for fear of crushing. So I kiss you and cuddle you.

The kissing is de-sexualized and is more akin to nuzzling. It is a kissing that is not conscious of time. When kissing leads to sexual arousal, it is as if a timing device has been activated.

According to Adam Phillips, in *On Kissing, Tickling and Being Bored* (1993): 'Adults tend to have strong, mostly private and embarrassed feelings about kissing.'

Don't adults tend to have strong, mostly private and embarrassed feelings about most things? Or would that just be me?

People say to you, 'What kissable lips'. But they don't kiss your lips. No one kisses you on the lips except my nan, who kisses everyone on the lips. She once kissed a friend of mine on the lips. He says she put her tongue in his mouth.

I have never been sure whether this story is true or not.

Kissing is a means of communication. As you get older you will kiss and not mean it. Ingrid Bergman, after the filming of *Casablanca*, said of Humphrey Bogart: 'I kissed him but I never knew him.'

knowledge

All knowledge is excessive. And most comes unexpected.

Einstein's wife was asked if she understood relativity: 'Oh, no,' she replied, 'although he has explained it to me many times – but it is not necessary to my happiness.'

There's stuff we don't need to know.

But all this information pouring into us, like a mighty torrent, like water hissing into dry sands. It's overwhelming. It's irresistible.

The older you get, the more desperate I become to learn facts, information I can pass on to you, things that you will need to know: Absolute Zero (273.16° Celsius, or 0° Kelvin, or 459.67° F). 100 per cent proof equals 52 per cent of alcohol by volume. Istanbul/Constantinople.

I would like to be able to give you a fully paid-up entrance ticket to European culture. Via the USA, Africa, Australia, the Poles, Russia, China, India and Asia.

Then, at other times, I think there's really nothing that you need to know. Nowhere you need to go. Nothing I can give you. Nothing I can teach you.

I have a fear, a dim awareness, that perhaps you know more about yourself and about us than you are letting on.

My mother-in-law asks, 'Do you think he remembers me?' I think you do.

laughter

When the first baby laughed for the first time, the
laugh broke into a thousand pieces and they all went
skipping about, and that was the beginning of fairies.

Peter Pan, J. M. Barrie, Act 1

Fairies are not funny.

Happiness is no laughing matter.

Baudelaire, in 'On the Essence of Laughter':

> human laughter is intimately linked with the accident of an
> ancient Fall, of a debasement both physical and moral.
> Laughter and grief are expressed by the organs in which the
> command and the knowledge of good and evil reside – I
> mean the eye and the mouth. In the earthly paradise . . .
> that is to say in the surroundings in which it seemed to
> man that all created things were good, joy did not find its
> dwelling in laughter. As no trouble afflicted him, man's
> countenance was simple and smooth, and the laughter
> which now shakes the nations never distorted the features of
> his face. Laughter and tears cannot make their appearance in
> the paradise of delights.

Pliny the Elder, in his *Natural History*, Book 7, writes: 'It is recorded of only one person, Zoroaster, that he laughed on the same day on which he was born, and also that his brain throbbed so violently as to dislodge a hand placed on his head – this foretelling his future knowledge.'

You laugh hysterically, building up to it.

Darwin, in *The Expression of Emotions in Man and Animals* (1872):

The sound of laughter is produced by a deep inspiration followed by short, interrupted, spasmodic contractions of the chest, and especially of the diaphragm ... From the shaking of the body, the head nods to and fro. The lower jaw often quivers up and down, as is likewise the case with some species of baboons, when they are much pleased.

Peekaboo works. Tickling doesn't.

lies

No one tells the truth about babies.

We learn to lie about you at an early stage.

H. L. Mencken, 'The Art Eternal': 'The more trivial, loathsome and degraded the reality, the more powerful and relentless must be the idealization.'

And vice versa.

Philip Larkin was right: happiness writes white.

l o n e l i n e s s

Like a dog, you're companionship. But also like a dog, you're not company.

love

A few months after your birth I begin to feel a total confusion. I am happy and I am sad. I am given to hyper-pessimism and hyper-optimism. The feelings seem to change from hour to hour, minute to minute. I feel ecstasy and I feel despair.

I suddenly remember that this is what it feels like to be in love.

Simone Weil: 'To love purely is to consent to distance, it is to adore the distance between ourselves and that which we love.'

Can you love?

Two answers. Hélène Cixous, in *Coming to Writing and Other Essays* (1991):

> In the beginning, I adored. What I adored was human. Not persons; not totalities, not defined and named beings. But signs. Flashes of being that glanced off me, kindling me. Lightning-like bursts that came to me: Look! I blazed up. And the sign withdrew. Vanished. While I burned on and consumed myself wholly. What had reached me, so powerfully cast from a human body, was Beauty: there was a face, with all the mysteries inscribed and preserved on it; I was before it, I sensed that there was a beyond, to which I

171

did not have access; an unlimited place. The look incited me and also forbade me enter; I was outside, in a state of animal watchfulness. A desire was seeking its home. I was that desire.

And Alice Thomas Ellis, in her book *Serpent on the Rock* (1994): 'I was once asked by a newspaper to write down a thought for Valentine's Day. I wrote, "Men love women, women love children, children love hamsters and hamsters don't love anybody."'

lullabies

Do you know any good lullabies?

I don't know any lullabies.

The only soothing tune I know is 'Goodnight Irene' –
Leadbelly – whose words are clearly unsuitable for tiny ears:
'Sometimes I live in the country / Sometimes I live in town /
Sometimes I have a great notion / To jump in the river and
drown.'

The only other songs I know are equally unsuitable pop
and rock: 'If I said you had a beautiful body would you
hold it against me?'; 'Welcome to the Hotel California';
'Psycho killer, fa fa fa fa, fa fa fa fa fa fa'; 'Should I stay or
should I go now? If I stay there will be trouble';
'Everybody was Kung Fu fighting. Those cats were fast as
lightning.'

I realize too late that I have been fatally infected by the times,
and that the symptoms are only now becoming apparent, in
parenthood.

I knew it. I should have paid more attention to Adorno's 'On
the Fetish Character in Music and the Regression of Listening'
(1938).

I know no whole songs. I can't even whistle a tune. (Whatever happened to whistling? Ronnie Ronalde – he was a music-hall artist – made a living as a whistler. My uncles used to whistle. Everyone used to whistle. It must have had something to do with trams and caps and cobbled streets.)

I check our CD collection and find to my surprise that we have Oasis, *Definitely Maybe*, REM, *Automatic for the People*, U2, *Zooropa* and *Achtung Baby*, and Nirvana, *Nevermind*. We also have Massive Attack, *Blue Lines*, Cornershop, *When I Was Born for the Seventh Time*, that Moby album, the Wu-Tang Clan, *36 Chambers* and Mary J. Blige, *What's the 411*.

Neither of us can remember buying any of these CDs and neither of us listens to any of them any more. The soundtracks of our lives no longer apply, and anyway, the songs are all unsingable, trite, and often meaningless. How did we get here?

Looking for something to sing, I find I have to dig much deeper, that I have to fall back on to other songs, remembered from other times, and I find to my astonishment that this does not mean that I am dredging up songs sung to me as a child by my own parents – nothing authentically ethnic, no 'Youghal Harbour' or 'The Croppy Boy', nothing Yiddish, not even an 'I'm Henery the Eighth I Am' or a 'You Don't Get Many Pimples on a Pound of Pickled Pork' – but rather that I am dredging up songs from *Joseph and His Amazing Technicolor Dreamcoat* and *Jesus Christ Superstar*.

Jesus Christ.

Whatever people say about Andrew Lloyd-Webber and Tim Rice, there's no doubt in my mind – it's memorable.

Like the taste of that slime they put in a Big Mac.

'Special' sauce.

To block out the interminable repetition of the colours of Joseph's coat – red and yellow and green and purple, and etcetera, all twenty-six of the bloody things – I often end up humming the tune to 'Danny Boy', or busking a couple of verses of 'Jerusalem', although I always seem to start in too low a key, so that by the time I get to the third and fourth verses, I'm growling.

Sometimes I make up songs, or at least chants, repeating phrases and putting new words to old tunes: 'Here's your milk, here's your milk, here's your milk', to the tune, to the drone, of 'Here We Go, Here We Go, Here We Go', and 'Oh No, Oh No, Oh No' to 'Olé, Olé, Olé, Olé, Olé, Olé', 'What Do We Want? We Want Milk? When Do We Want It? NOW!'

m a c h i n e s

From the first you are hooked on machines. You came into the
world with a clip on your head.

A friend lends us an automatic rocker.

You like it.

I hate it.

It feels like factory-farming.

manners

You know no manners.

You might almost be rich and famous. You are exempted from the usual rules of good behaviour.

You make me forget my manners. I shove past people with the buggy. I lose my temper with shopkeepers, bus drivers, pedestrians, and with the mothers at the mother and toddler groups.

A mother in a café is blowing big saliva bubbles at her baby. The baby seems to like it. I'm disgusted.

At a wedding I change your nappy in the church, on a pew. A man in a Panama hat and wearing a cravat gives me a funny look.

'All of us seem vulgar to someone,' wrote Louis MacNeice, 'In Defence of Vulgarity' (1937).

m e c o n i u m

When you are first born you pass something called meconium, which is smooth and a dark, dark green, almost black. It's a bit like caviar – black fish jam – and contains bile, mucus and digestive juices. Aristotle described it as 'unduly copious in comparison with the size of the child', which it is – very unduly – and midwives used to call it 'poppy-juice', which is exactly what it looks like: the rich slather of poppy-seed cake. In colour, writes Aristotle, it is 'extremely dark and pitch-like'.

The passing of meconium is one of the first shocking paradoxes of your being: a small, pink, dainty thing excreting a thick, dark pitch.

mementoes

Swedenborg's skull sold at Sotheby's in 1978 for £1,500 and George Bernard Shaw's gardening gloves for £28, Dickens's ivory pencil in 1977 for £110, Virginia Woolf's tortoise-shell glasses in 1980 for £250. Marilyn Monroe's certificate of conversion to Judaism went for $90,500 at Christie's in New York in 1999. Her brass-plated, ten-inch-tall menorah went for $19,500. Her prayer book fetched $46,000. Mary Anne Disraeli used to keep her husband's hair-trimmings.

What if we had Einstein's first shit? Wittgenstein's umbilical cord? A lock of hair of the baby Picasso, Pablito?

All mementoes are fakes.

'Fifty men could not carry the wood of what is called the true cross,' wrote Calvin.

Calvin didn't get it: all the bandages, the blood, the crowns of thorns, the cups, the grave clothes, the handkerchiefs, the nails, the reeds, the robes, the spears, the sponges and the whipping-posts, they're not remnants. They're souvenirs. Somewhere out there is the pap-dish and spoon used by the Virgin Mary. Or something similar.

Thomas Edison once said that genius was one per cent inspiration and ninety-nine per cent perspiration. Genius apart, my quota of inspiration came one Sunday twenty-five years ago, on 8 September 1963. I was in Inverness, mid-journey from Edinburgh to the very north of Scotland, when the pangs of hunger prompted me to find something to eat. My search ended with the purchase of a pack of Mackintosh's Munchies and a pack of McVitie's Ginger Nut biscuits, both from a vending machine as there were no shops open on a Sunday afternoon. It suddenly dawned on me, while consuming the Munchies, that when I threw the Munchies pack away, I would also be throwing away a small fragment of history.

Furthermore, the thought occurred to me that if I was to save the wrappers, tins and bottles from every product I bought, collectively they would represent a social history of life in Britain. I knew from my childhood experience of collecting Lesney 'Matchbox' miniature die-cast toys and from my research into philatelic postal stationery that there was continual change. Pack designs would be updated, new products would arrive, others disappear, and the advertisements for the products would tell of other aspects of social change. From that moment on I was to keep everything – for better or for worse.

Robert Opie, *Sweet Memories:
A Selection of Confectionery Delights* (1988)

We start with a shoebox.

memory

Memory is not a pocket.
Ralph Waldo Emerson

My first memory. The sound of mowers. The smell of pork
and gravy. Crumbs in the pocket of my father's dressing gown.

At the end of the year, it seems that I have forgotten
everything and can explain nothing.

I used to wonder why my parents could offer no sensible
advice about child-care. It was almost as if they had forgotten.

They had forgotten. Memory is as thin as the skin of a soapy
bubble.

> The more one learns, so to speak, the hang of oneself, and
> mounts one's problems, the less one is able to say what one
> has learned; not because you have forgotten what it was,
> but because nothing you said would seem like an answer or
> a solution: there is no longer any question or problem
> which your words would match.
> Stanley Cavell, *Must We Mean What We Say?* (1969)

Or, to put it another way:

It is this deep blankness is the real thing strange.
　　The more things happen to you the more you can't
　　　Tell or remember even what they were.

　The contradictions cover such a range.
　　The talk would talk and go so far aslant.
　　　You don't want madhouse and the whole thing there.
　　　　　　　　William Empson, 'Let It Go'

A friend says to me, why bother writing it all down? Does everything exist to be put in a book? Does it all have to be written down?

Yes.

And no. Not necessarily.

Elvis, according to his biographer Peter Guralnick, 'never kept a diary, left us with no memoirs, wrote scarcely any letters, and rarely submitted to interviews'.

But I'm not Elvis.

We forget everything, even the most important things.

Pascal, it is said, sewed a piece of parchment into his robe, as a reminder: 'In the year of Grace, 1654, Monday 23 November, from about half past ten in the evening till half past midnight.'

One afternoon, feeding you a bottle, there's a music documentary on the television, and they show a clip from *Jailhouse Rock*.

We even forget how Elvis dances.

milestones

Life is not a walk across a field.
Boris Pasternak

There is a concept of milestones in some of the child-care books, which is unhelpful. It implies that we are on a journey, and that life is a race from one post to another.

If this is a journey we are on a long detour.

But life is not a journey. Or a predicament.

Life is a joke. Seriously.

milk

Breast milk is 'expressed': it bears a signature.

Aristotle held the belief that breast milk was formed from menstrual blood. Galen called it 'white blood'.

It is living tissue. Its constituents are similar: protein, fat, carbohydrate, energy, cholesterol, vitamins A and C, Thiamin, Riboflavin, nicotinin acid, vitamins B6 and B12, folic acid, biotin, pantothenic acid, sodium, potassium, chloride, calcium, magnesium, phosphorus, iron, copper, zinc.

According to the scientific guide *Infant Feeding: The First Year* (1989), 'Differences in composition between preterm and term milk are explained by the probability of an alternative pathway for the secretion of substances from the blood, which involves some leakage of small molecules and ions between milk secreting cells and extracellular fluid (ECF).'

There are lots of bottles of milk in the fridge: cow's milk, breast milk and formula. The breast milk is by far the most sweet.

We're decorating. We run out of milk. It's too late to go to the garage.

Breast milk is OK in warm tea.

It is not so good on cereal.

Marina Warner, in her book on the myth and cult of the Virgin Mary, *Alone of All Her Sex* (1976):

> In the Old Testament, milk and honey form the twin images of the promised land, which to men and women of the New Covenant is the paradise of the afterlife . . . Neither milk nor honey requires any preparation to eat, but appears spontaneously in full perfection. No rites of purification attend their consumption: they are pristine. Eaten raw, they taste cooked. As symbols of nature's goodness, they are kin to sap and dew, which are also wild, but they are also nutritious in themselves. Unlike wine, another prime symbol of fertility and life, they undergo no process at the hand of man, and in their innocence are thus distinguished from other sources of nourishment. In the catalogue of effluvia milk therefore occupies a very different place.

Do you imbibe qualities of the mother through the milk? The Romans believed so.

Pierre Bourdieu:

> It is probably in tastes in *food* that one would find the strongest and most indelible mark of infant learning, the lessons which longest withstand the distancing or collapse of the native world and most durably maintain nostalgia for it. The native world is, above all, the maternal world, the world of primordial tastes and basic foods, of the archetypal relation to the archetypal cultural good, in which pleasure-giving is an integral part of pleasure and of the selective disposition towards pleasure which is acquired through pleasure.

mirrors

You look at yourself in the mirror. You do not smile. You cry.

You do not imitate us, we imitate you.

I have found myself more susceptible to tears and to rage since you were born. As if in some way your extraordinary behaviour legitimizes my own. Parents become like their babies: selfish, unmannered, often on the point of tears. (All these books about babies: so babyish.)

The mirror *is* terrifying – it displays our surfaces.

When you look at us, you seem to see through us.

Looking through the X-ray machine in Thomas Mann's *The Magic Mountain* (1924):

> Hans Castorp saw precisely what he must have expected, but what it is hardly permitted man to see, and what he had never thought it would be vouchsafed him to see: he looked into his own grave. The process of decay was forestalled by the powers of the light-ray, the flesh in which he walked disintegrated, annihilated, dissolved in vacant mist, and there within it was the finely turned skeleton of his own hand, the seal ring he had inherited from his grandfather hanging loose and black on the joint of his ring-finger – a

hard material object, with which man adorns the body that is fated to melt away beneath it, when it passes on to another flesh that can wear it for yet a little while . . . He gazed at this familiar part of his own body, and for the first time in his life he understood that he would die.

You illuminate also. Kevin Jackson, in his dictionary *The Language of Cinema* (1998), defines 'baby' in cinematographic terms: 'a small spotlight fitted with a 1,000-watt bulb used mainly for close-ups'.

Godard: 'Close-ups makes us anxious about things.'

We buy a full-length mirror. The long sad slow advance of our adult selves.

mobiles

We weren't going to bother. But. The views from the flat are not good. And Goethe:

> Eyes are educated from childhood on by the objects we see around us, a Venetian painter is bound to see the world as a brighter and gayer place than most people see it. We northerners who spend our lives in a drab and, because of the dirt and the dust, an uglier country where even reflected light is subdued, and who have, most of us, to live in cramped rooms – we cannot instinctively develop an eye which looks with such delight at the world.

I like it so much I want one of my own.

> A 'Mobile' Dimensions: 2 meters by 2.5 meters. Frame: 8 cm, flat red. The two white balls turn very quickly. The black spiral turns slowly and looks as if it were always ascending. The steel sheet rotates even more slowly, the two black lines look as if they were always ascending. The black pendulum, 40 cm in diameter, rises 45° on each side, going outside the frame in front, at the rate of 25 swings a minute.

Alexander Calder, statement to
accompany *Cadre rouge* (1932)

money

True or false? The children of the rich deserve better.

'Never mind the money,' I say, in discussion. We are paying for this with our lives.

I always mind the money.

A rich friend says, 'Babies are like yachts. People who have to worry about the cost shouldn't have them. Ha ha.'

Money makes you wise. It also makes you handsome. And, you know, you sing well too.

motherese

I just can't get the hang of motherese. (John Berryman was good at it.) I always feel embarrassed doing the voice and talking silly. It makes me feel like Princess Diana visiting a ward of the sick and the dying:

> Top of the Pops, Coronation Street, all the soap operas. You name it, I've watched it. The reason why I watch it so much now is not so much out of interest but if I go out and about, whether it be to Birmingham, Liverpool or Dorset, I can always pick up on a TV programme and you are on the same level. That I decided for myself. It works so well. Everybody watches it and I say: 'Did you see so and so? Wasn't it funny when this happened or that happened?' and you are immediately on the same level. You are not the princess and they the general public – it's the same level.
>
> quoted in Andrew Morton, Diana – Her True Story:
In Her Own Words (1997)

It's not the same level.

190

mothers

D. W. Winnicott, in the postscript to *The Child and the Family* (1957):

> Is not this contribution of the devoted mother unrecognized precisely because it is immense? If this contribution is accepted, it follows that every man or woman who is sane, every man or woman who has the feeling of being a person in the world, and for whom the world means something, every happy person, is in infinite debt to a woman. At the time when as an infant (male or female) this person knew nothing about dependence, there was absolute dependence.
>
> Once again, let me emphasize, the result of such recognition when it comes will not be gratitude or even praise. The result will be a lessening of a fear. If our society delays making full acknowledgement of this dependence, which is a historical fact in the initial stage of development of every individual, there must remain a block both to progress and to regression, a block that is based on fear. If there is not true recognition of the mother's part, then there must remain a vague fear of dependence. This fear will sometimes take the form of a fear of WOMAN, or fear of a woman, and at other times will

191

take less easily recognized forms, always including the fear of domination.

What can I say?

Thanks, Mum.

movement

In a higher world it is otherwise, but here below to
live is to change and to be perfect is to have
changed often.

Cardinal Newman, *Essay on the
Development of Christian Doctrine* (1878)

When first born, you have three basic positions: lying on your
back, on your side, on your belly. You cannot move from one
position to another.

Lying prone: knees tucked up under your tummy, bottom high
in the air, arms bent, head to one side.

Lying supine: head to one side, arms outstretched, one leg
outstretched.

Black's Medical Dictionary: 'For some weeks after an infant is born
the only signs of intelligence, apart from the performance of
the merely animal functions, consist in constant movements of
the lips, head, and limbs.'

You sit up, or at least slump forward, at about seventeen
weeks.

At seven months, you are able to roll on to your tummy from your back. You begin to press up with your arms. You start speeding around in the baby-walker, ramming closed doors.

Suddenly, our home becomes a dangerous place. We realize how dirty it is. There is dust everywhere. There are buttons and pins and biros on the floor.

Even when you start to walk you still don't stand up straight, or place your hands on the back of your hips, or raise your arms or interlace your hands, or hunch your shoulders, sit upright and relaxed, kneel, stoop, punch, sit cross-legged, kick without falling over, or crouch.

Sometimes, now you're walking, you're too excited to sleep. In the thirteenth and fourteenth centuries a dancing mania spread throughout central Europe: people danced until they fell, exhausted, or dashed out their brains.

You develop a safe cordon, which is about six feet in diameter. You will happily play within this area, and walk or crawl to its limits, but no further. You are like a goat or a dog tied to a stake.

You cock your head at my approach, like the velociraptor in *Jurassic Park*.

You roll around on the bed. You seem to enjoy it. Your body seems always to be moving.

Paul, Letter to the Romans, 7:21–4:

> My inner being delights in the law of God. But I see a different law at work in my body – a law that fights against the law which my mind approves of. It makes me a prisoner to the law of sin which is at work in my body.

What an unhappy man I am! Who will rescue me from this body that is taking me to my death?

Nietzsche, *Thus Spake Zarathustra* (1883): 'Behind your thoughts and feelings, my brother, there stands a mighty ruler, an unknown sage – whose name is self. In your body he dwells; he is your body.'

You seem to be moving in all directions at once.

From pram to stroller. From cot to chair. You move from Moses basket to cot, to chair, to pen, to nursery, to school, to work.

music

I can no longer listen to music with melodies. Except opera.

I prefer music whose principle is repetition. Dance music. Not just techno. Glenn Miller and his Orchestra. Benny Goodman before he became a trio.

Personally, I feel like I'm playing on a one-string fiddle.

m y t h s

I have to keep reminding myself that you are real.

The Renaissance concept of the king's two bodies, one
belonging to the terrestrial, the other to the symbolic sphere of
life.

You're not really here.

'The difficult task of knowing another soul is not for young
gentlemen whose consciousness is chiefly made up of their
own wishes' – George Eliot, *Middlemarch*.

naked

Kenneth Clark begins *The Nude* (1953):

> The English language, with its elaborate generosity,
> distinguishes between the naked and the nude. To be naked
> is to be deprived of our clothes and the word implies some
> of the embarrassment which most of us feel in that condition.
> The word nude, on the other hand, carries, in educated
> usage, no uncomfortable overtone. The vague image it
> projects into the mind is not of a huddled and defenceless
> body, but of a balanced, prosperous and confident body:
> the body re-formed.

You don't need re-forming. You're not nude. You're naked.

Eric Gill's book *Clothes* (subtitled *An Essay Upon the Nature and
Significance of the Natural and Artificial Integuments Worn by Men and
Women*), published in 1931, contains chapters on 'Clothes as
Houses', 'Clothes as Workshops' and 'Clothes as Churches and
Town-halls'. Gill argues that 'unlike a new-born rat or a
skinned rabbit, men and women, though without the things
we call clothes, are not necessarily what we call naked!' He
goes on:

> The human body is properly clothed in its skin; the skin
> itself is a suit of clothes, a body-fitting underwear, an

intimate garment . . . To see a man what we call naked is
like seeing a horse without harness, a tree without leaves,
iron without paint. It is the bed inside the curtains, the eye
behind the eyelash, the garden behind the wall. A 'naked'
man is clothed in silk – with hair in appropriate places, and
delicately ornamented with nipples and navel – a marvellous
mechanism of muscle and bone (more marvellous than that
of a horse, who can only run, or of a monkey, who can
only fool about) displayed and yet still covered.

I take you to a photographer for a portrait, a keepsake, for the
family. You're eight months old. You can sit up by yourself,
and you smile often and unprompted.

The photographer has a thin moustache and slicked-back hair.
He says he has seven children. His studio is in a shopping
centre, next to a McDonald's – the smell of hot meat and fries.

The photographer uses a feather duster on a long plastic stick
to make you smile and he takes a couple of shots, and then he
says to me, 'OK, you pop your shirt off, Dad, and we'll do a
nudey one. Just the two of you.'

I start to untuck myself, right there, in the window of the
shop, and then I notice a Ronald McDonald grinning at me,
and I stop.

No, thank you. I shall remain enrobed. This horse shall keep
its harness.

'You'll regret it,' says the photographer.

We go for milkshakes. I don't go back to collect the photos.

Sometimes people say, 'I could eat you up.' Like a confection.
This is usually when you are naked.

199

Cadbury's used to call the machine that coated their confections with chocolate the 'enrober'.

William Blake: 'When I feel very near God I always feel such a need to undress, as if everything which was artificial jarred me.'

You look more naked on a towel than off.

names

The Germans have -*chen*, -*lein* and -*schoen*. What do we have?

I don't want to tell anyone your name.

I want to keep it a secret. Your name appears on your birth certificate, but nowhere else. It occurs to me that no one need know. I don't want people to have that power over you. The beginning of *Dragnet*: 'Ladies and Gentlemen, the story you are about to see is true. Only the names have been changed to protect the innocent.'

I want to tell everyone your name.

I want to get hold of a sheet of A1, and spell out your name in some of that fine-spaced Gil Sans lettering, like the artist Richard Long. You're more interesting than some walk with stones.

I want to make a sign from Edward Johnston's Underground typography and put your name on the bar in the middle of a circle.

I want to inscribe it on rings and drinking cups. I want to paint it over the doors and on the doorposts of the house, and etch it in the glass of the windows.

I want strangers to point and to ask me.

When friends forget your name, I find it unforgivable.

When I forget the names of other people's children I find it funny.

Jerome K. Jerome, 'On Babies', from Idle Thoughts of an Idle Fellow (1886): 'If you desire to drain to the dregs the fullest cup of scorn and hatred that fellow human beings can pour out for you, let a young mother hear you call her dear baby "it".'

A man comes to fix the hole in the roof. His name is Steve Player. I make him coffee. He tells me that his real name is Bela Ishtan Rashko. He came over to England from Hungary in 1956. He was a first-division table-tennis player in Hungary. But now he's retired from professional sport. He's in his sixties. I ask him why he calls himself Steve Player. He says no one in England can be bothered with his Hungarian name, and then he says, 'Player. Geddit?' and laughs.

Writing to Rayner Heppenstall in 1940 from the village of Wallington, George Orwell (Eric Blair):

> Dear Rayner,
> Thousands of congratulations on the kid. I hope and trust both are doing well. Please give Margaret all the best and my congratulations. What a wonderful thing to have a kid of one's own, I've always wanted one so. But Rayner, don't afflict the poor little brat with a Celtic sort of name that nobody knows how to spell. She'll grow up psychic or something. People always grow up like their names. It took me nearly thirty years to work off the effects of being called Eric.

n a p

The single most beautiful word in the English language.

But a nap is not as good as a sleep.

Joseph Conrad retained his maritime habits, keeping the custom of four-hour rest periods.

nappies

In a terry nappy, or a linen one, you look classical, regal, Egyptian.

In a plastic nappy you look brutish, pre-packaged. Like a sandwich in a triangular pack.

On Ted Hughes, recalling their affair, Emma Tennant, in her *Burnt Diaries* (1999): '"I can't change nappies," Ted said. It was clear that this wasn't a failure of skills which he regretted: he was saying he can't and won't; and yet I've not asked him to do this, nor – if he had taken the trouble to find out – do I have a child young enough to need them.'

I meet someone who happens to be the cousin of a famous writer. The famous writer has several young children. Children loom large in his work. How does the famous writer cope, I ask the cousin. Oh, says the cousin, he doesn't do anything round the house. He doesn't have anything to do with the children.

There is undoubtedly something beautiful, as well as terrible, about your shits. It's not just the extraordinary colours, but also the shapes: they look like rough Rorschach ink-blots on the gauzy white surface of the nappy.

Shit is dirt, but it is also art: the nappy frames it.

Leo Steinberg, in *The Sexuality of Christ in Renaissance Art and in Modern Oblivion* (1984), argues that the loincloth in painted Crucifixions was a piece of 'compositional artifice'. 'It resolves a pictorial problem,' claims Steinberg, 'posed by conventional Crucifixion designs – the problem of vacant flanks in the middle zone of the field between crossbeam and horizon. By means of a gorgeous flutter flaring forth from the center, the blanks are repleted and animated.'

To the uneducated observer, there is another kind of symmetry at work: the loincloth Jesus wears in Crucifixion scenes looks suspiciously like the nappy he is often seen wearing in pictures of his birth, thus establishing a correspondence between womb and tomb, a line connecting his birth and death.

I say, 'Shall we keep one? As a memento. Just in case?'

Warhol autographed a sick bag on a flight from Miami to New York. It sold.

n a v e l

About a week after your birth you have your umbilical-cord clamp cut off.

The umbilical cord clamp is like a plastic clothes peg.

The useless cord itself bubbles up like a milky marble. Underneath it your belly button is on its way. It looks brown and bloody round the edges.

Freud claimed that dreams have navels, a spot that reaches down to the 'complex real'. And André Breton in the first *Surrealist Manifesto* (1924): 'It is perhaps childhood which comes closest to "true life".'

The stump is like a wound. It turns black and drops off. We throw it away, in the bin, with all our other rubbish: vegetable scrapings, milk cartons, slops, pizza crust. There'll be more: fingernails, scabs, hair.

We buy a bigger bin.

n c t

The plastic baby with the words 'DO NOT REMOVE' written in indelible ink on its belly. The letters are smudged.

needs

You're so direct it's terrifying. You do not allude to things. You do not suggest. You're like a rich man in a restaurant.

You are not subtle.

You're not dull.

INTERVIEWER: I've heard it remarked that your work is 'too sophisticated' for American readers, in that it offers no scenes of violence – and 'too subtle', in that its message is somewhat veiled. What do you say?

GREEN: Unlike the wilds of Texas, there is very little violence over here. A bit of child killing, of course, but no straight shootin'. After fifty, one ceases to digest; as someone once said: 'I just ferment my food now.' Most of us walk crabwise to meals and everything else. The oblique approach in middle age is the safest thing. The unusual at this period is to get anywhere at all – God damn!

INTERVIEWER: And how about 'subtle'?

GREEN: I don't follow. *Suttee*, as I understand it, is the suicide – now forbidden – of a Hindu wife on her husband's flaming bier. I don't want my wife to do that when my time comes – and with great respect, as I know her, she won't . . .

INTERVIEWER: I'm sorry, you misheard me; I said, 'subtle' – that the message was too subtle.

GREEN: Oh, subtle. How dull!

Terry Southern, interview with Henry Green, 1958, *Writers at Work: The Paris Review Interviews*, fifth series, ed. George Plimpton (1981)

night

I don't like the night, or early in the mornings. There are superstitions about the night: that fairies or witches or the Devil might carry babies away.

They're just superstitions.

But at night, even in the height of summer, I triple-lock the back door leading to the fire escape and shut the windows.

Feeding you at midnight, I feel connected with the whole world. I feel calm. W. S. Merwin, 'At Night', in *Houses and Travellers* (1977):

> Those who work at night are one body, and sometimes they are aware of their larger self. There are watchmen, helmsmen, surgeons, purveyors, thieves, bakers, mothers, beginners, and all the others. Together they are alive under the presence of the spaces of night, and it seems as though their veins might go on growing out of them into the dark sky, like a tree.

At night I lose my temper, like Wallace Stevens ('Anecdote of the Prince of Peacocks'):

In the moonlight
I met Berserk,
In the moonlight
On the bushy plain.
Oh, sharp he was
As the sleepless!

noise

At about seventeen weeks you discover your lungs and start shouting, rather than crying, and making whimpering noises, and something that sounds like babble. It is a kind of speech.

The visceral ejaculations, the hiccups, the burps, the retchings, the coos, the chuckles, the gurgles, the laughs, the squawks, they are all respiratory rather than oral. This is something new.

You scream.

Keats, in a letter to George and Georgiana Keats, 15 April 1819: 'The Servant has come for the little Browns this morning – they have been a toothache to me which I shall enjoy the riddance of – Their little voices are like wasps' stings.'

Your gurgling is towards yourself. One day you'll speak outwards, and eventually into strangeness.

And no one will listen.

'Streaming outwards,' writes George Steiner of language in *After Babel* (1975), 'it thins, losing energy and pressure as it reaches an alien speaker.'

Helmuth the Taciturn (Helmuth, Count von Moltke, 1800–1891) was reputed to be master of several languages, and never betrayed himself in any.

Your silence is not a decision; it is a state. You will never achieve that state again.

Always you will be expected to respond, and to initiate.

At eight months you start growling. You put things in your mouth – my old school recorder, the toilet-roll holder – and make the sound louder. I growl back at you, and for the first time we are talking. I growl, you growl, I growl, you growl.

It lasts for ten minutes before you give up (actually, I give up before you do).

It is a noise like Donald Duck crossed with a dog's growling. It makes you laugh.

You start to give little yelps and expulsions. We sit and do call and response.

It sounds like you're speaking Yiddish, or German.

You are asleep. I try a test of quietness: no radio. I can't cope.

nostalgia

We're already selling you back to yourself.

Crackling's not what it was.

nursery rhymes

The best nursery rhymes and lullabies have four-line stanzas and a strong andante beat. Also, it helps if there is a tone of menace and intimidation lurking under the surface.

Years ago, at a lunch-time seminar, a colleague spent the whole hour – while we were all busy eating our cold sausage rolls and warm yoghurts – trying to convince us that 'Roses are red, / Violets are blue. / Sugar is sweet. / And so are you' is all about rape, miscegenation and the slave trade.

A bit like the Police, 'Every Breath You Take'.

You could probably get a whole book out of 'Hush-a-bye, baby'.

obsession

We're obsessed. Some days we don't seem able to talk about anything else.

We breathe you.

> Euphoric or dysphoric states associated with emotion are, by and large, triggered by beliefs. Euphoric or dysphoric states associated with addiction are, by and large, triggered by the injection of a chemical substance and by its disappearance from the body. Although extremely different in origin, the phenomenology of the states can be quite similar . . . the subjective effects of amphetamine and of love are quite similar – not only the hedonic aspects but nonhedonic aspects as well, such as reduced need for sleep or food. The difference is that the person who is in love can only think about one thing, whereas amphetamines can enhance concentration on any activity. Sartre wrote *Critique de la raison dialectique* under its influence, and many students have taken it to write their term essays.
>
> Jon Elster, *Strong Feelings: Emotion, Addiction, and Human Behaviour* (1999)

parents

Parenting is an inadequately described occupation. Like parasitology.

'Anyone who hasn't had children doesn't know what life is' – Henry Miller, *My Life and Times* (1972).

All parents like to think they know what life is. The older the children, the more superior the parent.

Parents think they are proper, proper people.

They think they're professionals.

All parents are amateurs.

(The word 'amateur' is not an insult. Laurence Olivier called Marilyn Monroe a 'professional amateur'. A professional amateur is at least something. Olivier was a vile man who blacked up and put putty on his nose to play Jews.)

The parent belongs to a class. Only the rich escape being parents. Only the rich are not amateurs. The rich employ professionals.

The Amateur (someone who engages in painting, music, sport, science, without the spirit of mastery or competition), the Amateur renews his pleasure (*amator*; one who loves and loves again); he is anything but a hero (of creation, of performance); he establishes himself graciously (for nothing) in the signifier: in the immediately definitive substance of music, of painting; his praxis, usually, involves no rubato (that theft of the object for the sake of the attribute); he is – he will be perhaps – the counter-bourgeois artist.

Roland Barthes, *Roland Barthes* (1977)

Everybody blames their parents. We all of us like to think we started out from the wrong place. It makes life more interesting.

Parents are mysterious. They're like the court officials in Ryszard Kapuściński's *The Emperor* (1978):

Working as a protocol official in the Hall of Audiences, I noticed that, in general, assignment caused very basic physical changes in a man. This so fascinated me that I started to watch more closely. First, the whole figure of a man changes. What had been slender and trim-waisted now starts to become a square silhouette. It is a massive and solemn square: a symbol of the solemnity and weight of power. We can already see that this is not just anybody's silhouette, but that of visible dignity and responsibility. A slowing down of movements accompanies this change in the figure. A man who has been singled out by His Distinguished Majesty will not jump, run, frolic, or cut a caper. No. His step is solemn: he sets his feet firmly on the ground, bending his body slightly forward to show his determination to push through adversity, ordering precisely the movement of his hands so as to avoid nervous disorganized gesticulation. Furthermore, the facial features become solemn, almost stiffened, more worried and closed, but still capable of a momentary change to optimism or approval.

218

parks

Sitting in the park, noon on Monday, sky overcast, alone
except for you snoring in the buggy, the sound of children
playing, traffic, distant hammering, I have a momentary,
powerful sensation of freedom, of being without fear and
regardless of consequences, and am conscious of being, in
some irrational way, 'lucky'.

For a moment I think about getting up and walking away. This
is as good as it gets.

Instead, I feed the ducks and go to Boots to get some more
SMA Gold.

In the park, Sunday afternoon, feeding the ducks. The ducks
are all asleep. The water is black like oil and there is what
looks like a foamy white algae growing on the surface. It is
bread. The ducks seem to laugh as we leave.

In the park, pushing the swing, the mother next to me, older,
wearing a waistcoat of ecclesiastical embroidery, says, 'Isn't
this fun!'

In the park, pushing the swing, the mother next to me, half
my age, wearing a halter neck top, says, 'I'm not now with
the father of my child.'

In the park, three times in the course of the year, on a weekday, another father pushing the swing. Each time he is wearing a suit and tie. And each time — months apart — he says exactly the same thing to me: 'We drew the short straw today then.'

The park: an abundance of kindly and pleasant-faced people, the suburban lurking place of strangers.

past

The first six months seem to go slowly, then suddenly
everything speeds up and you are a year old and we are saying
to each other we must put those photos in an album, when
did he get his first teeth, when did she crawl? Where's that
shoebox?

Suddenly, you have a past. And so finally you are fully in the
present.

I promise not to talk about the past.

> Some people, whatever is happening *now*, either they
> can't handle it or they don't want to know. They'll be
> messed up on that bogus nostalgia thing. Nostalgia, shit!
> That's a pitiful concept. Because it's dead, it's safe — that's
> what that shit is about! Hell, no one wanted to hear us
> when we playin' jazz. Those days with Bird, Diz,
> 'Trane — some were good, some were miserable. But,
> see, people don't understand why I get so touchy
> sometimes. I just don't want to talk about that stuff.
> People didn't like that stuff then. Hell, why you think we
> were playin' clubs? No one wanted us on prime-time TV.
> The music wasn't getting across, you dig! Jazz is dead.

Goddamit. That's it. Finito! It's over and there is no point aping that shit.

Miles Davis, quoted in Nick Kent,
'Lightening Up with the Prince of Darkness:
Miles Davis Approaches Sixty', The Dark Stuff (1994)

Jazz is dead.

The shoebox is under the bed.

personality

The story is, Gershwin goes to Ravel and asks him for a lesson. Ravel says, why should you want to be a second-rate Ravel when you could be a first-rate Gershwin?

If you look at the early *Peanuts* cartoons Charlie Brown has not yet acquired his trademark jumper and his kiss curl is stuck to his head.

photographs

I've never taken so many photos.

We are constantly interrupting ourselves to take photos.

Susan Sontag, On Photography (1978): 'A photograph is not just an encounter between an event and a photographer, picture-taking is an event in itself, and one with ever more peremptory rights – to interfere with, to invade, or to ignore whatever is going on.'

We are trying to catch you out.

We are trying to explain your real self to your future self, to ourselves and to friends and family.

We are looking for something – just a glance. 'For there are mystically in our faces certain characters which carry in them the motto of our souls, wherein he that cannot read ABC may read our natures' – Thomas Browne, Religio Medici (1642).

Aged one, you make faces at the camera. I find it annoying. You are no longer innocent. 'Oh! please don't make such faces, my dear!' Alice begs the White King at the beginning of the Looking-glass story.

Brecht, 'The Lovely Fork':

> When the fork with the lovely horn handle broke
> It struck me that deep within it
> There must always have been a fault. With difficulty
> I summoned back to my memory
> My joy in its flawlessness.

People ask me if I have a photo of you in my wallet.

I haven't got a wallet.

piss

The sharp smell of your urine. It's refreshing. The smell of my own piss is disgusting. The smell of other people's piss also.

True story: 4.00 in the afternoon, Acton Town station. You are asleep in the buggy. A man with a moustache and wearing a leather jacket unzips his trousers and pisses on the platform. Trains go by. Commuters standing around. I do not pass comment. No one passes comment. I look away, check that you are still asleep, go back to reading the paper. The sound of pissing goes on for a long time.

True story: I'm drinking in a bar called Legends – it's a dump. It's 1.00 in the morning. There's a stag party in. They're in fancy dress. As I'm waiting for the Guinness to settle, the man next to me, dressed as Ali G, pulls down his canary-yellow jogging trousers, pisses in a pint glass and proceeds to drink it. There are cheers. I don't even bat an eyelid. The barman trims the Guinness with a knife.

Your piss smells so good I think about bottling it.

Andres Serrano has a *Piss Christ* (1987), a big Cibachrome photograph of a plastic crucifix dipped in a beaker of urine. He also has a *Piss Pope*, and an image of a Madonna and Child statue immersed in urine. The *Congressional Record* for 18 May

1989 records Senator Jesse Helms's objection to Serrano's work: 'Mr. President, . . . I do not know Mr. Andres Serrano, and I hope I never meet him because he is not an artist, he is a jerk'; Serrano responded to the attack in a letter to the chairman of the National Endowment for the Arts, arguing, 'My use of such bodily fluids as blood and urine in this context is parallel to Catholicism's obsession with "the body and blood of Christ".'

Serrano and Senator Helms deserve each other.

I wonder about exhibiting your every nappy since birth – nailing each one to a gallery wall, dating them.

And you know what?

The exhibition would be a sell-out.

plastic

The house is full of plastic and man-made fibres: spoons, cups, plates, bowls, bottles, toys, poly-cottons.

The character of plastic is unformed. It can take on multiple personalities.

Some friends swear by wood. But plastic seems appropriate. Wood is dead.

play

When I want you to play you do not want to play.

When you want to play I do not want to play.

This is another lesson.

Dr L. E. Holt's book *The Care and Feeding of Children*, first published in 1894: 'Babies under six months should never be played with; and the less of it at any time the better.'

presence

The first four weeks you seem precarious. You seem to be barely here. A part of you seems somewhere else.

But now you are unavoidable. You're everywhere. Like Boswell, who, according to Thomas Holcroft, 'obtruded himself everywhere'.

Evelyn Waugh, *Diaries*, 23 December 1946: 'The presence of my children affects me with deep weariness and depression. I do not see them until luncheon, as I have my breakfast alone in the library, and they are in fact well trained to avoid my part of the house; but I am aware of them from the moment I wake.'

You know what they say: Ireland is a great country to get a letter from.

pride

It is possible, even without taking pride in oneself, even while feeling utterly dejected, to take pride in one's children. This pride is a relief, and a pressure.

Coleridge, delighted, writing in his family Bible, sets up his son for a fall: 'September 19th, 1796. 30 minutes past two in the morning my Wife was delivered of a Son, his name Hartley Coleridge. N.B. He was born before either the Nurse or Surgeon arrived – & altogether without any aid.'

prizes

I feel as though I have been awarded a prize.

And I feel as though I deserve it.

But such a gift brings responsibilities. Jorge Luis Borges, winning a literary prize, bought the *Encyclopaedia Britannica* (eleventh edition). William Trevor gave some money to a school in Omagh.

A prize affords the opportunity to make amends.

Accepting the Goethe Prize in 1954, T. S. Eliot apologized for a hasty judgement ('Of Goethe perhaps it is truer to say that he dabbled in both philosophy and poetry and made no great success at either'), explaining, 'When a man is a good deal wiser than oneself, one does not complain that he is no wiser than he is.' You can take that as read.

pubs

The British go to pubs because their houses are so small. And to get drunk.

We no longer visit the pub. There's no point getting drunk.

It's like losing a room in the house.

George Orwell, writing about his favourite pub, the Moon under Water, in *The Evening Standard*, February 1946:

> The great surprise of the Moon under Water is its garden. You go through a narrow passage leading out of the saloon, and find yourself in a fairly large garden with plane trees under which there are little green tables with iron chairs round them. Up at one end of the garden there are swings and a chute for the children.
>
> On summer evenings there are family parties, and you sit under the plane trees having beer or draught cider to the tune of delighted squeals from children going down the chute. The prams with the younger children are parked near the gate.
>
> Many as are the virtues of the Moon under Water I think that the garden is its best feature, because it allows whole families to go there instead of Mum having to

stay at home and mind the baby while Dad goes out alone.

The only problem with the Moon under Water, as Orwell goes on to explain, is that it does not exist.

p u l s e

You have a higher normal heartbeat than an adult. I time it. It's about 120 beats per minute.

That's techno.

quiet

All these people coming and going. All this noise. The house is quiet only late at night and very early in the morning.

I know no privacy, only in my head.

When I think about all that quiet I wasted I could cry.

Sunday afternoon, at the out-of-town retail park, buying some plyboard to knock up a pelmet. There is a man, round about my age, sitting in his car, parked next to mine, eating a bar of chocolate, reading a men's magazine. I catch his eye.

radio

Imperceptibly, your routine begins to revolve around our listening habits.

In the mornings, I give you your breakfast at some time between the sports bulletin with Gary Richardson and 'Thought for the Day'.

'Good morning, Sue. Good morning, John. And good morning, all of you.'

I time your bath to coincide with *The Archers* and when you are still waking for your last feed we give you the feed just before *Book at Bedtime*.

I have rediscovered *On Your Farm*.

Telly's too demanding.

rebirth

The sense that you are an authorization for me to become what I am, which establishes my right to exist, to have a birth . . .

In having a child, you have your childhood returned to you, for better and for worse.

I explain all this to a friend. He says, 'God, don't go all New Agey on me.'

regrets

What can I say?

I wish we lived in a ground-floor flat.

religion

True or false? The whale swallowed Jonah.

We can't decide.

It's not the right question.

So how does one decide?

The minister in the hospital, speaking to the woman in the next bed. She is unmarried. Her child is twenty-four hours old. The minister says – and I quote – 'Well, you will have to take the responsibility for turning your back on God.'

An electrician comes to fix the trip switch and the ring circuit. He announces himself as a born-again Christian. He does a good job.

So that's 1–1.

I'm hedging. 'As for religion,' said Louis Armstrong, 'I'm a Baptist and a good friend of the Pope, and I always wear a Jewish star for luck.'

r e s e n t m e n t

I love my little son, and yet when he was ill
I could not confine myself to his bedside.
I was impatient of his squalid little needs,
His laboured breathing and the fretful way he cried
And longed for my wide range of interests again,
Whereas his mother sank without another care
To that dread level of nothing but life itself
And stayed day and night, till he was better, there.
Hugh MacDiarmid, 'The Two Parents' (1935)

Was Hugh MacDiarmid not a very nice man, or was he very honest?

Every day I find myself caught in little flurries of resentment.

We buy a camera with automatic red-eye reduction.

responsibility

Rabelais's last words are said to have been '*La farce est jouée*' ('The farce is ended').

We feel the same.

We're not funny any more.

ary, whether a family has religious views or
children into the religious life that is
at family. This usually involves special
en ancient in origin, whose function is to
nfant, and later, the adolescent, formally into
its responsibilities) as well as to explain the
peculiar to that sect.

cannot acquire beliefs at will. They require
just go out and buy a yarmulke or some
ion is about more than fried fish and

taste must be acquired, and like all other
e result of thought and the submissive study
s.'

ne necessary precipitate – like a death, or an
other tragedy.

e feel the need to dignify our lives.

rink wine and to take an interest in religion.

ieve: it's worth spending the extra pound,
door with a latch, by which persons may let

n, in his The Lives of the English Poets (1779–81):
ch is dangerous. Religion, of which the
t, and which is animated only by faith and
y degrees out of the mind unless it be
impressed by external ordinances, by stated
nd the salutary influence of example.'

observe are the purely practical: weaning;
ds; walking.

rest

There are two moments.

First thing, before you're awake ('The happiest part of a man's life is what he passes lying awake in bed in the morning,' writes Boswell in his *Journal of a Journey to the Hebrides*).

The moment after you go to sleep.

This is when we pull ourselves together.

restaurants

We are beginning to suffer from fear of restaurants: what
James Thurber calls 'Restauphobia'.

The nice restaurants don't want you. We are condemned to
canteens and Pizza Hut and McDonald's.

We say, it wouldn't be like this if we lived in Ireland, or Italy.

We move to Ireland. It's worse.

Television is our only common ritual: it supplies our need for participating in ritual and sharing beliefs about the meaning of life.

The only problem with television is that it does not aim at truth.

r o u t i n e

Tolstoy, writing about an illness: 'It was as if a wheel had seized me and were beginning to drag me into the machine.'

Routines are a kind of living death: I feel like a man facing a firing squad, hood over my head, a target hemmed over my heart. Ernst Bloch, *The Principle of Hope* (1959), vol. 1: 'The same things every day slowly kill us off.'

Routines are the only freedom. They are a necessary and almost a sufficient condition of success in any endeavour – you included. Goethe: 'Heaven gives us habits to take the place of happiness.'

We are constantly becoming accustomed, and then discomforted. We think you have established a routine – we accommodate ourselves accordingly – and then you change your mind.

Some friends don't believe in routine. Their toddler joins us for dinner one night. 'We don't like our lamb too fatty, do we?' they say. The toddler agrees. He's two. 'More wine?'

Everyone thinks their routine is the right one.

I wish there were a universal metronome.

'Are you one of these New Men then?' asks the born-again Christian plumber.

'I don't know,' I say.

'Well,' he says, 'I suppose everyone has to find their own way.'

I am lining up the keyhole with my belly-button and searching for middle C.

scrapbook

The scrapbook is half empty. Or half full, you say.

self

Do you know who you are? You contemplate, and sometimes we cannot stir you from your contemplation.

Are you having secret thoughts?

Your head is so large and so floppy, sometimes I think your neck might snap, like a cabbage-headed rose in the rain.

Hannah Arendt, *The Human Condition* (1958):

> One of the most persistent trends in modern philosophy since Descartes and perhaps its most original contribution to philosophy has been an exclusive concern with the self, as distinguished from the soul or person or man in general, an attempt to reduce all experiences, with the world as well as with other human beings, to experiences between man and himself.

You are reverse philosophy.

sentimentality

There is a pie in a story by Dickens, 'A Schoolboy's Story', which is described as having 'no flakiness in it'. It is solid 'like damp lead'.

I have developed a taste for heavy pies – the food of my own childhood.

I have always had a taste for bathos but I seem now to have acquired a taste also for schmaltz.

I could drink a gravy-boat of schmaltz.

I seem to have lost all reason. I will cry at almost anything, and not just John McCormack singing 'Danny Boy'. I am ready to be exploited by any child under the age of about sixteen, any con man, and anyone over sixty. I can no longer pass beggars on the street, or tin-rattlers, or miss ER. In the cinema we have to wait for all the credits to finish so I can wipe my eyes.

In telling stories about you we inevitably become the good little man or the good little woman maintaining our dignity in the face of trying circumstances. In our stories we become Deeply Emotional and Rather Delightful. There seems to be no avoiding this.

In our stories we do not shout or rant. To admit to this would be to rob our stories of their sentimental redemptive message. Make our stories into a cry for help.

Out with friends – all men, all single. There is smoke, and there is drink.

No matter how much I smoked or drank, I would still stink of Horlicks.

An open pie is a tart.

s e x

The shock of one's twenties: to discover that other people are as interested in sex as you are.

The shock of one's thirties: to discover that other people are as interested in babies as you are.

s h i t

A baby, in cockney rhyming slang, is a basin of gravy, which figures.

Gravy is brown and runny (or at least it's supposed to be runny: there's an old Tony Hancock sketch in which he says of his mother's gravy, 'At least it used to move around a bit').

Shit is baby browning.

For the first few months your shit is mostly the consistency and colour of wholegrain mustard, but sometimes it is greener, and sometimes blacker. It is never brown, and is more like paste than gravy.

When you move on to solids, your faeces change colour every day, according to what you've eaten (carrots – orange; spinach – green). We tend to read these shits, much as the ancient Etruscan haruspices examined chicken entrails to divine the future, or as maiden aunts read tea-leaves, and much as, every day, we read faces, anticipating response and reaction.

Of course, to read shits is to go the wrong way about things, 'as if a Traveller should go about to describe a *Palace*, when he had seen nothing but the *Privy*; or like certain Fortune-tellers in

Northern America, who have a Way of reading a Man's Destiny, by peeping in his *Breech*' – Jonathan Swift, 'Discourse Concerning the Mechanical Operation of the Spirit'. It's absurd, topsy-turvy, arse-about-face. But shit, nonetheless, demands a reading, and vice versa.

We are right, it seems, to read your shits. Green shit can be a sign of under- or overfeeding, and curds can indicate poorly digested proteins. Greasy shit indicates excess of fat or poor fat absorption. As parents we are glad when your shits are neither curdy nor greasy – a curdy or greasy shit being a kind of double negative, a dirt on dirt – and we tend to congratulate ourselves and, when you are first born, even congratulate you whenever you shit: 'Well done!' we say, peeling off another dirty, sodden nappy. 'Good boy!' The novelty soon wears off; after a while we no longer comment.

When you are first born you fart only quietly and your shitting makes no noise except for a slight popping and sussuration, the sound of sludge draining through a hole.

But as you get older your turds become a burden and you start to strain.

From about five months old, as the food thickens up, as you begin eating solids, you have to struggle to get it out. Your eyes bulge, you go bright red, your tongue sticks out, and your face is transformed into a mask, like a horrible grinning rictus. You grunt and groan.

Indeed, at times, shitting, you almost look like you could die; shit is, after all, 'morbid' matter, and defecation and urination are sometimes referred to as the 'eliminative functions', since they perform a role of casting out, and the phrase inevitably suggests also a sense of 'total' elimination, a sense of a hovering death in decay; thus 'crap', according to the OED, is 'Thieves' cant for the gallows, 'Hence crap v. trans., to hang'.

(And it happens, shit happens; people die taking a dump. Evelyn Waugh died on the toilet. Cicero's friend Titus Pomponius Atticus is said to have died from an affliction of tenesmus, 'A continual inclination to void the contents of the bowels or bladder, accompanied by straining, but with little or no discharge' (OED). According to the biographer Albert Goldman, Elvis Presley wore nappies in later life and died while he was sitting on the toilet, which is both pathetic and appropriate. Like singing in the shower, there's an intimacy, a close relationship, between shitting and singing; they're both performances which rely on careful control and expulsion. Enrico Caruso — if you like, the Elvis of opera — is supposed to have remarked, 'You know whatta you do when you shit? Singing, it's the same thing, only up!')

shock

We are all shocked, all the time.

Alexander Calder, describing his visit to Mondrian in 1930: 'The visit to Mondrian gave me the shock that converted me. It was like the baby being slapped to make his lungs start working.'

There are different kinds of shock, but they might roughly be divided into the pleasant and the unpleasant.

As an example of the unpleasant, Lord Justice Taylor's report on the Hillsborough Disaster, commenting on the food available at football grounds: 'The refreshments available to supporters are often limited and of indifferent quality. They are sold in surrounding streets from mobile carts and inside many grounds from other carts or from shoddy sheds. Fans eat their hamburgers or chips standing outside in all weathers. There is a prevailing stench of stewed onions.'

As an example of the pleasant, Henry James writing of coming to England in 1869 and finding 'an arrangement of things hanging together with a romantic rightness that had the force of a revelation'.

The shock of a baby lies somewhere between the shock of the stench of fried onions and the romantic rightness of a revelation.

shoes

We buy you your first pair of lace-up booties at seven months.

For the first time in my life I have started wearing trainers.

And for the first time in my life I desire a pair of hand-benched English shoes.

shops

Most shops cannot accommodate a double buggy.

There was a department store when I was growing up with wide aisles, and a pianist at Christmas.

But that was in Romford.

There is no music in Mothercare.

siblings

The only-child question arises.

Three years is about right. An interregnum.

A little time between two reigns.

I'm worried about feeling disappointed: like the depressing effect of the second bottle. There's no need.

You can never repeat yourself, no matter how hard you try, and it is a mistake to try and do so: Booker T and the MGs attempted for years to write more songs about onions.

sick

As the greenfly to the rose and the worm to the apple, so the tummy-bug to the baby.

One night, I am feeding you a bottle of milk, shitting on the toilet, having just vomited, crying, and I think, what have we come to?

My mum says, how often do you bleach your skirting boards?

I didn't know you had to bleach your skirting boards.

When you get sick, we're stuck with you. It's not like keeping pets. With parrots, when they get psittacosis, you can trade down to a budgie.

My dad says, it's funny, we never used to have all these things when you were little. My mum just raises her eyebrows. And he says, if you don't admit you have a cold it doesn't develop into one.

Chickenpox – the scars. I think, life is a history of damage.

silence

The occasional unexpected glorious flash of silence . . .

Like the great Modernists, and like Harold Pinter, you are a master of the ellipsis.

sincerity

Sincerity kills conversation.

I should know.

sitting

There was once an American Posture League.

You flop this way and that.

Your spine is like asparagus.

I feel like saying, 'Sit up straight! Don't slump!'

size

S. J. Perelman referred to his children as 'the dwarfs'.

You are like a dwarf.

Or an elf.

Or a goblin.

You look magical.

'Miniature,' according to Gaston Bachelard, 'is one of the refuges of greatness.'

Or, according to my dad, 'Thank goodness for small murphies.'

At around about a year old you suddenly change from looking like a dwarf (large head, saddle-shaped nose and round face, short thick legs and arms, inward curving back) to a midget (a miniature copy of a man).

To be honest, we do not want you to grow. Because it's true, what they say: tall men need midgets.

We'd like you to stay the way you are. But of course we can't keep you the way you are — unless we were to use a *gloottokoma*.

E. Tietze-Conrat, *Dwarfs and Jesters in Art* (1957): 'There is even a Greek word for the chests in which little children were locked up in order to hinder their growth, so that the lucrative career of a dwarf would be open to them: *gloottokoma*.'

You are like a mountain: always there.

skin

I cannot even begin to describe the colours of your skin. There
are too many subtleties of shade. It is peachy. Not in colour
but in texture.

There is not a mole, a boil, a wart, no pimples, freckles,
lumps, bumps, wens or goitres. There are, however, the
occasional sores and blemishes.

You tug at my neck: my skin is like leather, like a turkey, like
my grandmother.

Skin is an envelope containing you.

Or is it you?

Skin marks your boundary and measure. It is your measure.
Paul Valéry, 'Ce que l'homme a de plus profond, c'est sa peau' ('What is
deepest in man is his skin').

John Donne, Sermon XIV:

> In the outward beauty, These be the Records of velim,
> these be the parchmins, the endictments, and the evidences
> that shall condemn many of us, at the last day, our own
> skins; we have the book of God, the Law, written in our
> own hearts; we have the image of God imprinted in our

own souls; we have the character, and seal of God stamped in us, in our baptism; and, all this is bound up in this velim, in this parchmin, in this skin of ours, and we neglect book, and image, and character, and seal, and all for the covering.

sleep

You smile in your sleep, as you drop from one level of sleep to another.

At night we wrap you tightly in a white shawl, like a shroud, and lay you in a Moses basket, like a coffin.

Your face looks waxy when you sleep, and we check for life. We have to listen to you breathe, otherwise we cannot know that you live.

Slumped one night, asleep on the sofa, you look sluttish.

Every night you adopt the same posture: you lie with your right arm extended, your left hand curled into a fist. Your eyes look half-way open, like you're kidding. You whimper.

For the first four or six weeks you sleep a lot. Nearly twenty hours a day. Your waking and sleeping states are barely distinguishable.

At about nine months your sleeping becomes thicker: you do not rouse when we enter the room. Sometimes I panic; I have to prod you awake.

I wake up every morning feeling hungover – heavy and tired, with a coated tongue.

The last entry in the *Random House Dictionary*: 'zzz'.

smell

What is that baby smell in Johnson and Johnson baby oil?

In tests and polls people always say that they like the smell of babies, freshly cut grass, fresh cooked bread, roses and petrol.

The smellscape of our flat has changed. It smells milky. There is also a smell of shit. It is winter. We look forward to the summer, when we can keep the windows open. In the summer we discover that the windows have been painted shut.

When you are first born you have only two smells, or two sites of smell. First, the smell of the top of your head. Second, the smell of your bottom. I sniff the rest of you, but it doesn't seem to smell.

Some of the smells are intermittent, time-specific. When you've been fed, you smell milky, or what Michael Caine in *Alfie* calls 'milkified'.

You have been suffering from cradle cap. The health visitor says try olive oil. We anoint you every night. By morning you smell like rancidised chicken parts.

My grandad, who went in with the Allies to clear up Belsen,

would never talk about it. But he could not bear the smell of wine, or cheese. It reminded him, says my mum, of the stench of rotting flesh.

According to Plutarch, Alexander the Great smelled sweet.

I try to remember the smell of people I know and love.

I try to remember the smell of my own father: pipe tobacco, cut grass and flowers, coal-tar soap, shaving cream, brilliantine, eggs and bacon, lard, sweat, wood, petrol, no garlic. This doesn't even come close.

Susanne Langer, in *Feeling and Form* (1953), writes about 'the good and bad odors of words, which interfere with their strict meanings'. The odour of the word baby is both sweet and sour.

smile

You start to smile at around three months. With a stroke around the face, or by smiling at you close up, it's guaranteed.

Friends say, 'You should always smile at your baby.' These are friends who have never had a baby.

It's easy to smile at a baby for five or ten minutes a day, but all day, or for an hour?

A lot of the time, I don't smile. A lot of the time I frown.

Smiling hurts.

When you smile the corners of your mouth crinkle upwards, your mouth turns into a Cupid's bow. It is what is called a 'Duchenne' smile, named after a Frenchman: an eye-crinkling grin which involves the whole face.

You have a croissant-shaped smile.

For the weekend, for a treat, I buy a four-pack, from the supermarket, 'All Butter Croissants'. They're crushed, so they're marked down.

snot

A furrow of snot running from nose to mouth.

solids

At six months you start eating Weetabix for breakfast. You love Weetabix. Weetabix is a kind of pap.

Valerie A. Fildes in *Breasts, Bottles and Babies: A History of Infant Feeding* (1986):

> The main foods used for mixed feeding during the period 1500–1800 were pap and panada, or variants of these. Pap was said to date from the mid-15th century, and consisted of flour or breadcrumbs cooked in water or milk; panada was of more ancient origin, and consisted of bread, broth (sometimes with legumes, oil or butter) or milk; eggs were occasionally added.

You eat toast and crackers: crispy crunchy food. It is returned like ectoplasm.

We give you mashed-up potato, baby rice, pear, banana, and apple. Courgette and carrot. We purée the foods, put them in ice trays, and then in freezer bags, taking a small block for each meal and defrosting it in a cup of hot water.

We wipe the spoon along your upper lip, on your top palate: we are scraping food into your mouth, almost as if we were scraping dirt from our shoes, or excess margarine from the

275

knife back into the tub.

Oddly, at first, your shits don't smell. Your urine is astringent, and sprays far, but not the shit: it tends to stay in the nappy, and is odourless.

But once you start on solids the shit begins to spread, and to smell: of bad ham, of chicken, of rotting vegetables and, increasingly, damp straw (this distinctively shitty smell deriving from the organic compound *skatole*).

That's life.

We do not feed you salt. Salt and sugar are bad.

We also do not feed you sausages, corned beef, anchovies, pickles or olives. We're not offering you deep flavours.

In *A History of Food* (1992), Maguelonne Toussaint-Samat writes that a truffle-hunting sow must never be trained with second-grade truffles, or she will develop a taste for them and ignore the best.

speech

You don't. But it doesn't seem to be to your disadvantage.
There are other ways of being explicit.

You make language seem like an optional extra.

There are two talking animals in the Bible: the serpent and
Balaam's ass.

strangers

I go to a party. I am introduced by the host to someone who has also recently had a baby. Apart from that fact, we have nothing in common. We have nothing to talk about. We struggle for a few moments, exchanging and comparing basic baby information: age, sex, sleeping patterns. Then we give up and go our separate ways, find other people to talk to, people with whom we have something in common.

For a moment, when you are born – in the delivery room, and for a few weeks after, we feel connected with the whole world. And then we remember: everybody is a stranger.

We go on holiday, go abroad. Women stop us on trains and speak to you. Children come up to you and play with you. People talk to us, and laugh with us. We get on the plane to come back to England. The plane is full of Brits. No one speaks to us or to you. The man sitting next to us ignores you completely, even when you have your fingers in his ear.

As you get older, you become invisible. The only time your presence is remarked upon and congratulated is on polling day for the parliamentary elections.

We are in the hall of a Baptist church. It's 11.00 in the morning. Old men and women are lining up behind and in front to cast their vote. They talk to you: 'Going to vote?' 'Who are you going to vote for?' 'First election?' We're like one big happy family.

In the booth I make my mark. None of the candidates is really suitable.

stuff

Stuff, Junk . . . General terms for opium and all
derivatives of opium: morphine, heroin, Dilaudid,
pantopon, codeine, dionine.

William Burroughs, *Junkie* (1953)

We have become addicted to stuff.

But to catch a whale you need a harpoon.

sugar

I know I shouldn't, but sometimes a lick of honey does the trick.

I remember my own father's speciality: sugar sandwiches, with or without condensed milk.

supermarkets

My most meaningful conversations take place with the women at the supermarket checkouts.

One day, you're nearly a year old and I'm talking to the woman at the till. I haven't seen her before.

She's middle-aged. You're smiling and showing off your teeth. The woman is swiping. I am buying nappies, wipes, jars, Kleenex, coffee, biscuits, crackers and cheese. Just the basics. The woman pauses and asks how old you are. I tell her, and then I ask, to be polite, 'Have you had a good day?' She tells me, yes, it was OK, thank you for asking.

Then she says, do you believe in the power of prayer?

I say I don't know.

She says she believes in the power of prayer, because she had just been praying that someone nice would come along. This is her first day on the tills. She says, I'm a full-time carer, then she corrects herself. *Was* a full-time carer. For twenty years.

Her son died in May.

She says she's lucky to have the job here, really, isn't she? The people are very rude.

superstition

My mother – who is not a gypsy – insists on crossing your palm with silver. She gives you a tiny five-pence coin. People used to give babies eggs, salt and bread. (*Notes and Queries*, 5th series, 1878, explains: 'In Lincolnshire, at the first visit of a new baby at a friendly house, it is presented with an egg, both meat and drink; salt, which savours everything; bread, the staff of life; a match, to light it through the world; and a coin, that it may never want money.')

surprise

Sydney Smith, in a letter to Francis Jeffrey in 1805, describes his wife as 'as pregnant as the Trojan Horse'.

A baby is an exclamation mark.

swaddling

And she brought forth her first-born son, and
wrapped him in swaddling clothes, and laid him in
a manger.

Luke 2:7

Clothes and clothing don't really matter much in the Bible;
they function mostly as symbols, being torn or stripped or
cast off.

Joseph's coat of many colours, for example – despite Tim Rice
and Andrew Lloyd-Webber – gets only one brief mention and
then is gone ('they stript Joseph out his coat, his coat of many
colours that was on him').

The Bible's a funny book like that; there's almost a complete
lack of realistic detail: no one coughs or sneezes (apart from
the Shunammite's son, 2 Kings 4: 35), there's no mention of
annoying personal habits, and there's hardly any convincing
dialogue.

But why should there be? Eric Auerbach argues in *Mimesis*
(1946, translated 1953) that to expect such details is to miss
the point. Biblical narrative, according to Auerbach, unlike that

of the Greek epics, 'was not primarily oriented toward "realism" . . . it was oriented toward truth'.

Even in the New Testament, clothes are put on and put up with only in the interest of truth. Jesus mentions clothes only once or twice, and only then to press home a point: in Matthew 6:28 he asks, 'And why take ye thought for raiment? Consider the lilies of the field, how they grow; they toil not, neither do they spin.'

What is swaddling? Diana Dick, in her book *Yesterday's Babies: A History of Childcare* (1987), describes it in detail:

> The child was first cleaned with wine or warm water, and a little capon grease or vegetable oil was rubbed on its bottom to prevent a nappy rash. Linen cloths, called tail clouts, were placed over the buttocks, and then the baby was dressed in a open-fronted vest or jacket. A folded piece of linen called a 'bed' encased the trunk and legs . . . Having arranged the infant in its vest and 'bed', the business of swaddling now began.
>
> Rolls of cloth were wound first round the waist, and then diagonally down towards the feet and back again. Similar bands encircled the chest, and when the baby's arms had been placed straight down by its side, these were in turn bound to the already swaddled trunk. A cotton cap, with a pad to protect the fontanelle, was placed on the head, and two further caps put on top of this for greater warmth. To the top of this outermost cap, a strip of linen called a stayband was attached, and when the two ends were pinned to the front of the swaddled chest, it effectively prevented the infant from moving its head from side to side. A cushion, or small mattress, was laid under the child at this stage, and this in turn secured with still more binding to its

body. This solid unbending package, which had started out as a small baby, was now almost ready. Although, even then, it was not thought to be completely dressed until it had been covered with a blanket – regardless of the season. By the time the nurse had completed her task, only the child's face was exposed to the air – and even this was commonly covered with a veil, when it lay asleep in its cradle or was taken out of doors.

Swaddling was a means of pressing the baby into shape: moulding it into quietude and preparing it for adulthood.

In the West we don't swaddle our babies any more.

We exert other pressures.

swallow

Babies swallow like gulping fish.

swimming

We travel by bus to the swimming pool.

You sink. I fish you out.

Swimmers on the way home, at the bus stop. One person is eating a Kentucky, one is smoking. 'It goes down so well,' she explains. Her hair is still wet. One man says that he nearly drowned once, years ago, and had to spend three days in Penzance General Hospital.

You have all this to look forward to.

sympathy

A friend says, 'Fine. But what about the daily pressures of investment banking?' I'm really not interested.

It's difficult to feel sympathy for anyone.

Lord Berners's folly displayed the notice, 'Members of the Public committing suicide from this tower do so at their own risk.'

t a l k

Sometimes I can't be bothered to talk to you. I think, it's like feeding pigs with cherries. What's the point?

But remember, not all communication is talking, say the baby books.

But remember, not all talking is communication.

In a shop, you in the buggy, I go to leave, and I say to the shopkeeper, with an exaggerated hand gesture, 'BYE-BYE! BYE-BYE!' I am speaking for you.

My intonation is becoming more melodic. I have started to speak so clearly and so slowly that I am almost articulating my punctuation marks. Stop!

teeth

I am escaped with the skin of my teeth.
                                    Job 19:20

Your first tooth. It looks like a piece of china, or a piece of porcelain, like a sliver of fingernail growing out of your mouth. It makes you cry and dribble. You get dribble sores – red marks on your chin.

Cynthia Ozick, in *The Shawl* (1980), describes a baby tooth as 'an elfin tombstone of white marble', an image that works on two levels. Baby teeth don't just look like tombstones, they act like tombstones: your teeth commemorate a passing-away.

Pathologists sometimes use a method known as fluorine dating: dating skeletal remains from the amount of fluorine in teeth; after death it decreases at a known rate.

We escape by the skin of our teeth (a phrase that always puts my teeth on edge, like the thought of custard skin, and the skin on tea).

The first tooth is soon accompanied by a second, and when they both break through they're like two fangs poking up out of your bottom lip, dead centre. The left-hand tooth (your left, our right) grows slightly quicker than the other. I imagine the years of orthodonty.

I sing you soothing songs, but it makes no difference. 'Music helps not the toothache' – George Herbert, 'Jacula Prudentum'.

television

I watch television programmes which feature young children and babies in hospital. I cry.

We allow you to watch TV – or at least sit slumped before it – but we worry about it. We think we should be talking to you instead.

The television is a baby-sitter.

Kojak, played by Telly Savalas: 'Who loves ya, baby?'

It's not the content. The content is irrelevant.

When we visit people in their homes, they keep watching television, or keep it on. When I was young it wasn't polite to have the TV on with guests in the house. You still feel like a guest, someone who must be attended to – you're not yet family, someone who can be ignored.

George Gerbner's Cultural Indicators Project reckons that the average American child will have witnessed more than 8,000 murders and 10,000 other violent acts on television by the time he or she leaves elementary school. Gerbner: 'Whoever tells most of the stories to most of the people most of the time has effectively assumed the role of parent and school . . . teaching us most of what we know in common about life and society.'

It's a beautiful summer's evening and I'm pushing you in the buggy to get you to sleep. The streets are deserted. Total silence. The only sign of human life, inside the houses: the flickering of television screens.

We are shadowed by television.

terror

It's as if someone has sent us something nasty in the post. Or something nice. You are the gift and the sender.

thinking

Like a man who spends all day lying in bed, the muscles of his limbs turning to fat, my mind turns to mush. Like the inside of a summer fruit.

Yes, I want to say to friends who use hair-care products and buy new books, I am as stupid as I look. These *are* jumbo cords.

I stare at your profound forehead. All babies are born intellectuals.

You are living the life of the mind.

Mine.

tidying

You're messy.

Jackson Pollock, that painting, *Full Fathom Five*, full of detritus: nails, a key, buttons, coins, a cigarette, drawing pins. Now I get it: the mess, the excitement, the huge continent.

There's no way the English could have come up with Abstract Expressionism.

(The English did come up with Abstract Expressionism: Turner.)

There's no end to the tidying.

Some projects are simply doomed to failure: there's a story that Marilyn Monroe ran herself to exhaustion picking up fish – which fishermen had left on the sand because they could not sell them – and throwing them back into the sea.

I attempt to disinfect the skirting boards.

Any place housing a baby would be best skimmed over with concrete and clad with titanium walls, like the Guggenheim museum in Bilbao.

t i m e

'They're not little for long,' says my mother-in-law.

It's interminable.

> There was much discussion of just how long Adam and Eve
> spent in Paradise on the first and only day there. The
> rabbinic tradition, for example, had Adam and Eve expelled
> twelve hours after God first assembled the dust to create
> Adam. In *The Table Talk*, Luther imagined the creation of
> Adam at midday and the expulsion two hours later. To John
> Calvin, Adam sinned at noon and was called to account at
> sunset. Andrew Willet had Adam and Eve defending
> themselves early in the evening, around eight or nine hours
> after Adam's creation. Giovanno Loredano allowed Adam
> only three hours of happiness, a reminder to us all of the
> fleetingness of pleasure: 'About three o'clock he was
> brought into the Garden; at six a clock, he sinned; and in
> the Evening, was expulsed. In a word, Humane felicities are
> no other than moments. They for the most part find their
> Coffin in their Cradle, and their death in their birth.'
>
> Philip C. Almond, *Adam and Eve in*
> *Seventeenth-Century Thought* (1999)

I tell myself I'm not really a parent. I'm only doing this for the
time being. Until something else turns up.

tired

Life, according to Henry James, 'is effort, unremittingly repeated'. He was understating. Life is one long process of getting tired.

We're worn out.

'My dear Sir, a presentiment is on me, – I shall at last be worn out and perish, like an old nutmeg-grater, grated to pieces by the constant attrition of the wood, that is, the nutmeg' – Herman Melville, letter to Nathaniel Hawthorne, 1? June 1851.

toes

At six months, you lie on your back, sucking your toes. For some reason I find this thrilling and scary.

My sister says, 'Should he be able to do that?'

You are *uroboros*, the serpent eating his own tail. You have made a complete circle.

The sweet smell of your feet: so delicious, so disgusting. (Ernest Hemingway couldn't think of a suitable description for Wyndham Lewis: 'toe-jam' was the best he could do. That's perfect.)

tongue

Your tongue moves like wind on grass.

touch

We touch you in ways we would touch no other – we stroke your bottom, ceaselessly – and we expect no other to touch you in the same way.

The poet Anthony Hecht writes about touch: '"Touch" is a kind of black quartz or jasper, whose full name, "touchstone", derives from its use in testing the purity of gold or silver by rubbing them upon its polished surface.'

You seem to enjoy being naked. You seem to enjoy the surface of your body.

Diane Ackerman, in *A Natural History of the Senses* (1990):

> An odd feature of touch is that it doesn't always have to be performed by another person, or even by a living thing. A maternity hospital in Cambridge, England, discovered that if a premature baby were just placed on a lamb's-wool blanket for a day it would gain an average of fifteen grams more than usual. This was not due to additional heat from the blanket, since the ward was kept warm, but more akin to the tradition of 'swaddling' infants, which increases tactile stimulation, decreases stress, and makes them feel lightly cuddled. In other experiments, snug-fitting blankets or clothes reduced the infants' heart rate, relaxed them; they slept more often in their womblike bindings.

toys

You have to discard the toy in order to get at the box and the shiny paper.

travel

It's not worth it.

We fly to visit relatives. The luxury of drinking on the plane. I ask for a Bloody Mary. There is no tomato juice. But I can have another complimentary bag of nuts. That's nice, says the woman next to me. She doesn't understand.

She tells me that her dog is in the hold, and she's very worried. They don't put babies in the hold, do they? No, I agree. She is vegetarian. She gets meat. She makes a big fuss.

t r u t h

A true account of the actual is the rarest poetry.
Henry David Thoreau

But you can't make a living from telling the truth.

Voltaire on St Zapata: 'He isolated truth from falsehood and
separated religion from fanaticism. He taught and practised
virtue. He was gentle, benevolent and modest and was roasted
at Valladolid in the year of grace, 1631.'

Flying to America you have to fill in a questionnaire. Question
c reads:

> Have you ever been or are you now involved in
> espionage or sabotage; or in terrorist activities; or
> genocide; or between 1933 and 1945 were you involved,
> in any way, in persecutions associated with Nazi Germany
> or its allies?

What can you say?

I don't know anything about you.

You don't know anything about me.

I don't know anything about myself.

The truth about babies?

Not this.

No enlightenment. No epiphanies. Tumult. Tranquillity.

t u p p e r w a r e

We buy Tupperware.

I thank God daily for Earl Silas Tupper and his flexible, lightweight containers.

Leftovers can be tasty.

umbilicus

The windings of the umbilical cord are due to your moving and twisting in the womb. I didn't know.

According to Valerie A. Fildes in *Breasts, Bottles and Babies: A History of Infant Feeding*, in ancient India,

> Before the cord was cut, the mouth of the new-born baby was cleaned with ghee (clarified butter) and rock salt. Then, as part of the immediate post-natal rites, it was given an electuary of honey, clarified butter, and the expressed juice of Brahmi leaves and Anatá, mixed with a little gold dust, and given with the ring finger of the feeder.

The midwife snips it.

It looks like a huge tail.

'For the benefit of the scientifically inclined,' writes Ferdinand Gonzalez-Crussi in his *Notes of an Anatomist* (1985), 'here is a recent update on *Homo caudatus*':

> This was the only catch of the Boston Children's Hospital Medical Center between 1936 and 1982, noted in an article published in the prestigious *New England Journal of Medicine*. A healthy baby was born with a tail that measured 5.5 cm in length by 0.7 cm in diameter at its base, tapering toward

the tip, and emerged 1.5 cm to the right of the midline adjacent to the sacrum; histological examination showed it to be composed of skin tissues only, having neither cartilage nor bone. To the casual observer it looked like a large and well-formed tail. But it was boneless and off-center. Thus, in the best scientific tradition it was pronounced a tail and not a tail. The scholarly discussion in the report is admirable in its breadth, summoning arguments from embryology, bio-chemistry, genetics, and comparative anatomy. In the course of the discussion it is mentioned that, from the standpoint of molecular biology, we are closer to our tailed animal brethren than we would like to think. Thus, there is an astounding similarity between human and chimpanzee DNA, as there is between the chimpanzee's genome and that of other primates, including tailed monkeys. If we are phenotypically different, it seems, we owe it to regulatory genes rather than structural genes. In the best scientific tradition, it is concluded that the appearance of a tail in a human baby should be interpreted as a regression and not a regression.

vaccinations

Already the state governs your body. As Anthony Synnott puts it in *The Body Social: Symbolism, Self and Society* (1993): 'The year 1853 . . . marks a turning-point in the political anatomy of the body in England: i.e. in the relation between the body physical and the body politic.' In 1853 the government passed legislation making smallpox vaccinations compulsory for all children.

violence

There has only been once. You were three months old and were still feeding through the night every two to three hours.

I go into the bedroom to calm you and feed you. You refuse to feed and refuse to be calmed. I walk up and down with you. It doesn't work. I walk up and down with you even faster. Eventually I am jogging you up and down, and begin to shake you. You stop crying. I realize what I am doing. I stop shaking. I lay you down in your cot and walk out of the room.

I am ashamed. I don't tell anyone.

voice

The kite once had a different voice, a voice which was high-pitched and shrill. But one day he heard a horse neighing beautifully, and he longed to imitate it. Try as he might, he simply couldn't attain the same voice as the horse, and at the same time he lost his own.

This is why he has neither his own voice nor that of the horse.

Jealous people envy qualities which they don't possess and lose their own.

The Complete Fables, Aesop, translated
Olivia and Robert Temple (1998)

A woman in a pub – Lorraine – says to me, 'Where are you from?' I say I'm from Essex. 'That's not an Essex accent,' she says. 'That's mockney.'

Everyone's accent is constructed.

vomit

Having a baby is to be like Jonah, to be alive, but to be somehow vomited back into life.

In the maternity ward, the woman in the next bed is holding her new-born baby, cooing. She's just been feeding her a bottle of formula. The baby projectile-vomits.

'Aaaghh!' screams the woman. 'Exorcist!'

waking

You often wake up before your face, and your face still shows the night: it is moon-shaped.

And now, when you wake up, you don't immediately start crying. You lie awake, looking up at the ceiling, wriggling in your shawl, rocking from side to side, staring straight ahead. And you smile when I go to pick you up for the morning feed.

walking

You concentrate as you pull yourself up, bending your legs. Your legs seem triple-jointed. You are able to move in all directions. You move fast. You fall over a lot.

Every lunch-time I sit and eat my sandwich and look outside, opposite, where a man has his fruit and veg stall on the corner of a busy road.

Every lunch-time the man goes across the road to the bank to deposit his morning's takings. He runs across the road and runs back again.

This lunch-time as he runs across the road he falls, but gets up again. A car just misses him. He's lucky.

People pay good money to see other people fall over: sport, comedy, sex. You're so funny when you fall over, it could almost be a performance.

Norman Wisdom, on falling over: 'I get bruises frequently, but I think about the money and I'm soon all right.'

Walking involves a spatial reconfiguring, a change in how one thinks about places, an opening of different places and spaces within oneself: new compartments, chambers, rooms, both literally and etcetera.

My father-in-law takes you out in the buggy for the first time.
We walk down to the beach together, to the place near the
pub where his father was a deck-chair attendant, many years
before. The deck-chair attendant's hut has long gone, but my
father-in-law stands on the spot where it once stood, and we
take a photograph, of you, him and the concrete, and then we
walk home.

waste

The waste, even in a fortunate life.

In the modern industrialized West, an adult's shits are flushed away, but a baby's shits are buried. First it goes in bin-bags. Three or four or five nappies a day, wrapped, often, in fragranced nappy sacks. Why?

Why don't we use terry nappies, or something more environmentally friendly?

We are lazy, obviously.

But also because it is satisfying to dispose of a shit by wrapping it up and throwing it away.

The flush toilet long ago removed the pleasure in expulsion famously depicted in Hogarth's *Night* (a picture that is itself satisfying for a number of reasons: the returning drunk who gets doused with a pailful of shit is the then-notoriously unpopular magistrate, Sir Thomas de Veil). G. M. Trevelyan, in his *English Social History* (1944), describing the disposal of 'night-soil':

> Far overhead the windows opened, five, six, or ten storeys in the air, and the close-stools of Edinburgh discharged the collected filth of the last twenty-four hours into the street. It

was good manners for those above to cry, 'Gardy-loo!' (*Gardez l'eau*) before throwing. The returning roysterer cried back, 'Haud yer hand', and ran with humped shoulders, lucky if his vast and expensive full-bottomed wig was not put out of action by a cataract of filth.

Trevelyan's use of the phrase 'full-bottomed': proof that historians have a sense of humour.

You can even buy the 'Sangenic Nappy Disposal Unit', which wraps up to eighteen nappies in 'clean fragranced film'.

water

At about four months we feed you water. You seem to like the taste. I'm surprised, after all that milk – doesn't it seem thin? But you lap it up.

It's necessary.

According to several sources, W. H. Auden believed his greatest success was to have been quoted by a prostitute in prison complaining about the infrequency of showers. She quoted a line from his poem 'First Things First': 'Thousands have lived without love, not one without water.'

I resolve to drink my two litres a day.

weaning

In Kazakhstan babies are weaned on camel's hump, ram's tail boiled in milk and the neck fat from horses.

weight

When you are born everyone asks what's your weight.

There's nothing else they can ask.

They never ask again.

You are eight months old. I am reading a very long novel. The book's dust-jacket tells me that the author is a genius. I persevere. The book uses long sentences, complex narrative devices and includes many learned and cryptic allusions to ancient myths and legends.

I am balancing the book on my knee while shovelling food into your mouth, redirecting streams of food and dribble.

What is genius scared of?

A fall into the feminine, the minor. The domestic.

When I have wiped you down with a dirty J-cloth, shaken off the excess and unravelled you from the high-chair, I hoist you up on to my shoulder, and even with a full meal inside you, and – ah, yes – a full nappy, you are as light as a feather.

All those literary guys hanging round the heavyweight boxers – Mailer, Baldwin, Budd Schulberg, Ben Hecht. Isn't that troubling?

The average weight of cremated human remains is about ten pounds. That's about three pounds heavier than a new-born baby.

white

When you are first born – for, say, the first two months – we dress you mostly in white.

This seems natural and inevitable, but it wasn't until the mid-eighteenth century that plain linen became widely available as a fabric for clothes.

White is not a colour. It's a revelation.

I remember my nan, who saw the snow on the lawn at my mum and dad's last Christmas – you were newly born – and she said to me and my sister, amazed, 'The green is all white.'

White is neutral. It contains all colours.

White is a screen. It allows us to imagine you in any way necessary. In a letter Captain Scott addressed to his wife on 1 January 1911, a letter that was never sent and was found with his body, he wrote:

> On all sides an expanse of snow-covered floes, a dull grey sky shedding fleecy snow flakes, every rope and spar had its little white deposit like the sugaring on a cake. A group of penguins were having highly amusing antics close by, and the sounds of revelry followed behind, but

on the white curtain of feathery crystals I tried to picture your face, and I said God bless her for having been an unselfish wife, and the best of friends to an undeserving man . . .

w o m b

A woman wearing white, sitting at a desk behind protective glass, hands us a small brown envelope. We give her £2. We move along, away from the queues and stand together, shoulder to shoulder, in the shadows of a long corridor, and we slowly open the envelope and look at the pictures inside.

The ultra-sound scan looks like a satellite picture of the earth, with you constellated in the middle in black and white and grey. We receive one free copy and then it's £1 each for extras.

We are still in the corridor. I take a peek at my watch. I have to get back to work. I say, 'Don't you have to get back to work?'

Sometimes I have a strange feeling that you ante-date your birth, that we have somehow plucked you out of the ether, where you already happily existed. I ask some friends with children, they say they sometimes think the same.

On the scan you look like an astronaut, like Neil Armstrong on an old black and white telly, somersaulting in the amniotic fluid, forehead first, mouth open.

I say, shame it's a bit blurred.

Nabokov was more interested in life before birth than life after death: the embryo, 'the tiny madman in his padded cell'.

In *Speak, Memory* (1967):

> I know . . . of a sensitive youth who experienced something like panic when looking for the first time at some old home-made movies that had been taken a few weeks before his birth. He saw a world that was practically unchanged – the same house, the same people – and then realized that he did not exist there at all and that nobody mourned his absence.

Actually, you can miss something or someone without knowing what you're missing. You can mourn an absence without a loss.

It is frightening and bewildering to imagine life in the womb – the little paddles turning into hands, the muscles and tendons attaching themselves to the skeleton, the growing of lips, then the eye muscles, the neck, then the shoulders, the arms, the trunk, the legs and feet.

Thinking and writing about it make you seem monstrous.

It makes you sound strange.

But you know, you are strange.

words

Words pounding at you. Words even on your clothes.

The words on your clothes are either babyish slogans or brand-names.

We try to avoid too much branding, which makes you into a kind of bill-poster, one of Dickens's famous walking adverts, 'a piece of human flesh between two slices of paste board'.

Oscar Wilde defended street-advertising, with its adverts for pills and soap, because, he said, 'They bring colour into the drab monotony of the English streets.'

But you're not drab.

The single most common word currently found on children's clothes expresses a deficiency, a lack, almost a signal that the clothes mean more than the child: GAP.

Some of the other phrases are painfully self-referential. You have a pair of dungarees which bear the legend 'I look cute in this'. A lot of the words are related to animals and animal behaviour, and are printed in eccentric typography, often mixing upper and lower case, or reversing and transposing letters.

Eccentric typography in writing by adults is a sign of lunacy or dyslexia, but on clothes for children it's acceptable – it's as if the baby or child has written it on the clothes themselves. We are making you write the words we would like you to write. Dogs and cats figure large in both word and image: happy doggies, BeaR brothers, cissY cAt, The DoG, LUCKY DOG, all star puppy.

Pet.

They're primitive: pictographs, petroglyphs, rebuses. Like Lascaux, Les Combarelles, Font de Gaume, Niaux.

The words are for us to see and for other people to see. Like uniforms, they're signs that we – and through us, you – are behaving appropriately. They work like labels, labels that read 'BABY'.

We seem to need reminding that you are a baby.

work

There are no part-time babies.

I tell a colleague that we are having a baby. She says, 'That's your career over then.'

I laugh.

She's right.

'I must frankly own, that if I had known, beforehand, that this book would have cost me the labour which it has, I should never have been courageous enough to commence it' – Mrs Beeton, preface to her *Book of Household Management* (1861).

There are no small jobs.

worry

Worry is like rolling your eyes. It has no purpose.

You're eleven months old, and my grandad comes to me in a dream one night.

In the dream I'm cooking — and I can't get my puddings right.

I ask him what I'm doing wrong. He says, 'Your pudding string's too tight.'

y o u

We are not alone.
Close Encounters of the Third Kind

You are not me.

Seven Ways to Treat a Person as a Thing

Instrumentality. The objectifier treats the object as a tool of his or her purposes.

Denial of autonomy. The objectifier treats the object as lacking in autonomy and self-determination.

Inertness. The objectifier treats the object as lacking in agency, and perhaps also in activity.

Fungibility. The objectifier treats the object as interchangeable (a) with other objects of the same type and/or (b) with objects of other types.

Violability. The objectifier treats the object as lacking in boundary integrity, as something that it is permissible to break up, smash, break into.

Ownership. The objectifier treats the object as something that is owned by another, can be bought or sold, etc.

Denial of subjectivity. The objectifier treats the object as something whose experience and feelings (if any) need not be taken into account.

Martha C. Nussbaum, *Sex and Social Justice* (1999)

zero

A cup of tea and a slice of chocolate cake, spotted with wax, and the year's gone.

Like snow in the hand.

You're one.

acknowledgements

I owe a debt of gratitude to the following, who have offered encouragement, assistance, friendship and/or financial support during the writing of this book. Some of them are dead. Most of them are strangers. A few of them are baby-sitters. The famous are not friends. None of them bears any responsibility:

Peter Abelard, AC/DC, John Adams, Theodor Adorno, Sajidah Ahmad, Pedro Almodovar, Claire Armitstead, W. H. Auden, St Augustine, Jane Austen, Paul Auster, Johann Sebastian Bach, Francis Bacon, Nicholson Baker, Honoré de Balzac, the staff of Bangor Public Library, Iain Banks, John Banville, Jonathan Barker, Paul Barker, Michael Barrymore, Jacques Barzun, Count Basie, Suzanne Beard, Samuel Beckett, the staff of Belfast Central Library, Saul Bellow, Alan Bennett, John Berger, John Berryman, George Best, William Blake, Ernst Bloch, Aleksandr Blok, Caroline Blyth, the staff of the Bodleian Library, Marc Bolan, Bono, The Boomtown Rats, James Boswell, Robert Boyers, Billy Bragg, Joshua Brand and John Falsey, Bertolt Brecht, Chris Bristow, the staff of the British Library, Tony Bromham, Benjamin Britten, Julie Burchill, Kenneth Burke, T-Bone Burnett, Ron Butlin, David Byrne, J. J. Cale, Maria Callas, Italo Calvino, the staff of Cambridge University Library, Enrico Caruso, Johnny Cash, Stanley Cavell, Miguel de Cervantes, Ray Charles,

Geoffrey Chaucer, John Cheever, Noam Chomsky, Christo,
John Clare, The Clash, Bruce Cockburn, Leonard Cohen,
Norman Cohn, Samuel Taylor Coleridge, John Coltrane, Eddie
Condon, Abi Cooper, Joseph Cornell, William Cowper, Richard
Crashaw, Dante Alighieri, Robertson Davies, Miles Davis, Ray
Davis, Robert De Niro, Philip K. Dick, Charles Dickens, Emily
Dickinson, Tommy Dorsey, Fyodor Dostoevsky, Ian Dury, Bob
Dylan, Robert Edwards, George Eliot, Ralph Waldo Emerson,
Emerson, Lake and Palmer, Eminem, the Master, Fellows and
staff of Emmanuel College, Cambridge, William Empson, Brian
Eno, Erasmus, Euripides, William Faulkner, Giles Foden, Peter
Forbes, Michael Frayn, Sigmund Freud, Robert Frost, Sinéad
Garrigan, Marvin Gaye, George Gershwin, Ira Gershwin,
Johann Wolfgang von Goethe, William Golding, Benny
Goodman, Muffin Gordon, Alasdair Gray, David Gray, Christine
Greathead, Michael Greathead, Al Green, Clement Greenberg,
Miriam Gross, Tony Hancock, William Hanna and Joseph
Barbera, The Happy Mondays, Jeremy Harding, Thomas Hardy,
the staff of Harlow Public Library, John Hartley, Daniel Hatter,
David Herd, George Herbert, Zbigniew Herbert, Rebecca
Herrisone, Eva Hoffman, William Hogarth, Billie Holiday, Sally
Holland, Sara Holloway, Homer, Bohumil Hrabal, Dan Hunter,
Nicholas Humphrey, Rachel Humphreys, Jack Hylton and his
Orchestra, Elin ap Hywel, Henrik Ibsen, Gail Ingram, James
Ingram, Ivan Illich, J. B. Jackson, Jeremy Jacobson, Harry
James and his Orchestra, Henry James, William James, Randall
Jarrell, Martin Jones, Rowena Jones, Franz Kafka, Mary Kay-
Wilmers, Brian Keenan, Garrison Keillor, Peter Kelly, James
Kelman, Harry Kemelman, Tim Kendall, John Kerrigan,
Rudyard Kipling, Paul Laity, William Langland, Philip Larkin,
Primo Levi, Clarice Lispector, Toby Litt, Leon Litvack, Emanuel
Litvinoff, Alan Lomax, the staff of the London Library, Richard
Long, Alan Lovell, Glen Lovell, Helena Lovell, Lisa Lovell,

Shirley Lovell, Gail Lynch, Phil Lynott, Gustav Mahler, David Mamet, Bob Marley, Charbel Mattar, Fiona Matthews, John McCormack, Mike McKie, Louis MacNeice, Herman Melville, H. L. Mencken, Peter Menell, John Milton, Charles Mingus, Amedeo Modigliani, Christy Moore, Marianne Moore, Alberto Moravia, Sir Thomas More, Wolfgang Amadeus Mozart, Ron Mueck, Paul Muldoon, Iris Murdoch, Anna Murphy, Pablo Neruda, New Order, Robert Nibbs, Friedrich Nietzsche, Flann O'Brien, Sinéad O'Connor, Frank O'Hara, Bridget O'Rourke, Ovid, Amos Oz, Cynthia Ozick, Al Pacino, Arvo Pärt, Blaise Pascal, Boris Pasternak, Walter Pater, Tina Perfrement, Harold Pinter, Plato, Jackson Pollock, Vasko Popa, Sally Potter, Elvis Presley, Michael Prodger, Giacomo Puccini, François Rabelais, Mark Radcliff, John Redmond, Lou Reed, Django Reinhardt, Charles Reznikoff, Ernest Ridley, Florence Ridley, Arthur Rimbaud, Peter Robinson, the staff of Romford Public Library, Gillian Rose, Joseph Roth, Philip Roth, Salman Rushdie, Ray Ryan, Vera Ryhazlo, Deborah Sansom, Eileen Sansom, George Sansom, Rhoda Sansom, Ted Sansom, Francis Schaeffer, Michael Schmidt, Martin Scorsese, Jon Scourfield, William Shakespeare, Rangeley Shallis, James Shivers, Stephanie Shivers, Jacqueline Simms, Frank Sinatra, Iain Sinclair, Isaac Bashevis Singer, Josef Škvorecký, Andy Small, Stevie Smith, Sophocles, Francesca Spranzi, Atima Srivastava, Saviana Stanescu, Saul Steinberg, Laurence Sterne, Jonathan Swift, Paul Tabrett, Andrey Tarkovsky, Art Tatum, Margaret Thatcher, James Thurber, Andrew Todd, William Trevor, King Tubby, Giuseppe Verdi, Claire Vincent, Dave Vincent, Virgil, Tom Waits, Jr. Walker and the All Stars, Chick Webb, Ben Webster, John Webster, Cornel West, Andy White, William Carlos Williams, Jah Wobble, Estelle Wong, Jessica Wong, Louise Wong, Norman Wong, Rachel Wong, Mark Wormald, Malcolm X, Neil Young, Zounds.

CHEMISTRY
Damien Wilkins

The Webb family seem genetically disposed towards medicine. Don, the eldest brother, runs a small town pharmacy. Penny, the abused wife, neglectful mother and firebrand sister, is a doctor. And Jamie, the youngest son, who hasn't been back to their small town in New Zealand for twenty years, has been self-medicating with heroin for longer than seems physically possible. And then Jamie moves back home, setting off a chemical reaction in his dysfunctional family which has disastrous consequences.

'A terrifically good book, so cleverly constructed and managed. It's a work of real tenderness . . . powerful and convincing'
Jim Crace

'An engrossing, tender and sad story told in a fiercely energetic prose that very rarely loses momentum . . . This is the kind of novel the British public sorely needs'
Niall Griffiths, *Big Issue*

THE FUNNIES
J. Robert Lennon

In his weekly comic strip, Carl Mix immortalized his family as a loving group of wisecracking imps. When he dies, his estate is divided between four of his children – in reality a dysfunctional, semi-estranged brood. The fifth, Tim, a struggling artist, is given three months to draw the strip. If he succeeds (giving up his own work) he will have inherited a gold mine; if he fails, he will get nothing.

This brilliant portrait of a family, each member tyrannized by their cartoon alter egos, secures the renown of an immensely gifted young writer.

'A poignant, wry novel, with laugh-out-loud moments'
Independent

'A brilliant book'
Marie Claire

'A particularly satisfying tale of a family wrecked and partially reassembled by cartooning . . . neatly executed, with unpretentious intelligence'
Financial Times